10 LANGUAGES
You'll Need Most in the
CLASSROOM

A Guide to Communicating With English Language Learners and Their Families

Garth Sundem ~ Jan Krieger ~ Kristi Pikiewicz

CORWIN PRESS
A SAGE Company
Thousand Oaks, CA 91320

Copyright © 2008 by Corwin Press

For information:

Corwin Press
A SAGE Company
2455 Teller Road
Thousand Oaks, California 91320
www.corwinpress.com

SAGE Ltd.
1 Oliver's Yard
55 City Road
London EC1Y 1SP
United Kingdom

SAGE India Pvt. Ltd.
B 1/I 1 Mohan Cooperative Industrial
   Area
Mathura Road, New Delhi 110 044
India

SAGE Asia-Pacific Pte. Ltd.
33 Pekin Street #02-01
Far East Square
Singapore 048763

Printed in the United States of America

Library of Congress Cataloging-in-Publication Data

Sundem, Garth.
Ten languages you'll need most in the classroom : a guide to communicating with English language learners and their families / Garth Sundem, Jan Krieger, Kristi Pikiewicz.
        p. cm.
Includes bibliographical references and index.
ISBN 978-1-4129-3781-8 (cloth)
ISBN 978-1-4129-3782-5 (pbk.)
    1. English language—Study and teaching—Foreign speakers—United States—Handbooks, manuals, etc. 2. English teachers—Training of—United States—Handbooks, manuals, etc. I. Krieger, Jan. II. Pikiewicz, Kristi. III. Title.

PE1128.A2S8872 2008
428.2'4—dc22   2007033945

This book is printed on acid-free paper.

11   12   10   9   8   7   6   5   4   3   2

Acquisitions Editor:	Rachel Livsey
Managing Editor:	Cathy Hernandez
Editorial Assistants:	Megan Bedell & Ena Rosen
Production Editor:	Catherine M. Chilton
Copy Editor:	Ann Lloyd
Typesetter:	C&M Digitals (P) Ltd.
Proofreader:	Sally M. Scott
Cover Designer:	Lisa Miller
Interior Illustrator:	Ron Carboni

10 LANGUAGES

You'll Need Most in the

CLASSROOM

Contents

Preface

The face of your classroom is changing. According to the U.S. Department of Education, more than five million English Language Learner (ELL) students were enrolled in public schools in 2003. This is more than double the number found in 1990, representing a rate of increase seven times that of total school enrollment (National Clearinghouse for English Language Acquisition and Language Instruction Educational Programs, 2006). And while the majority of these ELL students speak Spanish, this is changing as well (Meyer, 2004). In today's classroom, you might use Korean in the morning, Russian in the afternoon, and Arabic tomorrow. Even if you don't currently have students who speak the ten languages in this book, the chances are you soon will. And it might take only one or two words from you to show your new students that they are appreciated in your classroom, school, and community.

This book offers the resources you need to communicate, at least on a very basic level, with students from the ten most common non-English-speaking populations in U.S. classrooms. With picture dictionaries, content area vocabulary, and translated reading level assessments you can support your students at school; with reproducible parent letters you can bridge the all-important gap with home.

The ten languages in this book are not the ten most common in classrooms. But they are the most common for students *who do not also speak English*. Thus Hmong, Haitian Creole, and Cantonese are included, while French, German, and Mandarin are not. This distinction might seem small, but it speaks to the purpose of this book: you can use it to communicate when English is not an option.

While communication may be the most obvious of your challenges in teaching ELL students, it is probably not your only goal. Supporting your students who are struggling with culture shock and the difficulties of adjusting to a new school, country, and potentially a new family may also be important to you. To help you learn about your new students and connect with them, this book offers quick information about your students' countries of origin. With your compassion and these communication aids, you can help ELL students learn to respect their individuality while getting up to speed in the classroom as quickly as possible.

Publisher's Acknowledgments

Corwin Press gratefully acknowledges the contributions of the following reviewers:

Becky Castro, Project Director
Montebello Unified School District, Montebello, CA

Ann C. Edmonds, Consultant
Clayton School District, Clayton, MO

Mary Enright, Assistant Principal
PS/MS 4, Bronx, NY

Thomas S. C. Farrell, Professor of Applied Linguistics and
    Department Chair
Brock University, St. Catharines, Ontario, Canada

Johanna Haver, Independent Education Consultant and Author
Phoenix, AZ

Tery J. Medina, Associate Director
The Southeastern Equity Center, Fort Lauderdale, FL

Nenita Pambid Domingo, Asian Languages and Cultures Lecturer
University of California, Los Angeles

Gay Q. Yuen, Professor of Education
California State University, Los Angeles

Deborah A. Zeis, Teacher
Charlotte Middle School, Charlotte, MI

About the Authors

 **Garth Sundem**, MM, is an author and teacher trainer, and has published more than twenty books, primarily on the subjects of literacy and social studies. He graduated magna cum laude from Cornell University and earned a master's degree in music theory and composition. Titles of which he is especially proud include *The Doggy Dung Disaster: And Other True Stories of Regular Kids Doing Heroic Things* (Free Spirit Press, 2006), *Implementing an Effective Writing Program Using the Traits of Good Writing* (Teacher Created Materials, 2004), and *Geek Logik: 50 Foolproof Equations for Everyday Life* (Workman Publishing, 2006).

 **Jan Krieger**, MEd, has worked as a multicultural educator for many years, teaching at bilingual schools throughout Mexico and Central and South America, as well as in the United States, where he has taught Spanish at both the middle and high school levels in Bozeman, Montana. He was recently selected as a Fulbright Exchange Teacher and taught English as a second language in Cuernavaca, Mexico. His master's degree is in curriculum and instruction with an emphasis in multicultural education. Before teaching, he worked as a wilderness guide, fishing guide, mountain bike guide, and field researcher in Alaska; directed the Yellowstone Youth Conservation Corps; was a ski patroller in Argentina; and has led adventure trips in Tahiti, the Galapagos Islands, and the Amazon region. Every year, he leads groups of language students to Spain, France, and Germany.

 **Kristi Pikiewicz** is a middle school social studies and language arts teacher, author, and frequent presenter at local, state, and national conferences. Her first teaching position was at Hill Middle School in Novato, California where she was hired by the Bay Area School Reform Collaborative to work as a Title I Literacy Specialist in an area where many students were learning English as a second language. She continues to value multiculturalism and hands-on learning in her classroom. Ms. Pikiewicz holds a BS in environmental science with a minor in political science and is finishing her PhD in Clinical Psychology.

Introduction

HOW TO USE THIS BOOK

While this book will be useful to the ELL professional, it is meant for the general K-12 teacher who has encountered or may encounter English Language Learner students in the classroom. A chapter is included for each of the ten languages most spoken by students who do not also speak English, beginning with the most common language and proceeding to the least common one. Each chapter includes the following resources:

- *Country of Origin Information*—Use this country and culture information to connect with ELL students and to show your appreciation for and interest in students' cultural backgrounds. Perhaps you will have a small celebration on an important holiday, or ask ELL students to share their traditions or religion with the rest of the class.
- *Useful Phrases*—Refer to these in basic communication with students and families. Included are words and phrases specifically useful in the school setting.
- *Student Dictionaries*—Use these reproducible picture dictionaries in the classroom, on the playground, and in content-area classes. You can copy and post these pages in your classroom to aid communication between your ELL students and the rest of the class. Encourage your English-speaking students as well as your ELL students to review these dictionaries.
- *Parent Letters*—It is likely that the parents of ELL students also speak little English, making the all-important communication with home difficult. Use these translated, reproducible parent letters to convey both caring and concern.

The reading tests included in Chapter 11 are *very* basic and do not replace the more detailed evaluations that will be administered by your district's ELL services. However, until these services are put in place, these tests can give you a basic picture of a student's reading skills (and prior schooling). Use them to determine if an ELL student struggles due to language unfamiliarity or to reading difficulties, and adjust your lessons and expectations accordingly.

With this book, the motivated mainstream teacher can open the channels of communication with English Language Learners and help these students feel like an appreciated part of your classroom and school community.

GENERAL TEACHING TIPS FOR USE WITH ELL STUDENTS

Respect Cultural Differences

The etiquette of communication and societal norms varies across cultures. Differences in appropriate eye contact, male/female relationships, and physical space can lead teachers to incorrectly interpret student behavior (Ortiz, 1995). Be aware of putting students in situations that are outside their cultural comfort zones but also be aware of the potential to stereotype your students based on cultural expectations. This, of course, is a fine line that you will need to tread with care. By learning as much as you can about an ELL student's background and culture, you can take steps toward creating a supportive and sensitive environment that is conducive to learning.

Below are some generalizations to keep in mind when exploring interactions with your new students:

- Many cultures see eye contact as aggressive or intimate (especially between the genders).
- Spanish-speaking, Arabic-speaking, and Asian students may be comfortable with less personal space and more physical contact than students (and teachers) experienced with American culture. Asian students, however, may be very uncomfortable being touched on the head.
- Korean families may place extreme importance on education and can become upset by the appearance of their child's underachievement.
- Parents of Asian students relate to teachers more formally than do their American counterparts.
- Spanish-speaking students might offer immediate respect for females in authority roles while withholding respect from female peers.
- Arabic-speaking students may have difficulties with females making decisions and exercising authority.
- Nodding and saying "yes" in Asian cultures demonstrates hearing but not necessarily agreement.
- Spanish-speaking students may prioritize family obligations over education.
- Copying schoolwork may be acceptable to students from former Eastern-bloc countries.
- Students from Asian countries might excel in memorization but have difficulties with reading comprehension.

Use Nonverbal Cues

When language fails, resort to strategies such as pictures, objects, demonstrations, gestures, and intonation cues (Northwest Regional Educational Laboratory, 2003). For example, you might point to the bookshelf when saying, "Please choose a book." Be creative, kind, and persistent in getting your point across. Once a student has learned language basics, try to extend this language by using it in conjunction with nonverbal cues.

Encourage Partnering

If there are students who speak the same language as a new ELL student, consider asking the more fluent in English to help the less fluent. If your ELL student is the only speaker of his or her language, assign a responsible student to help the English learner navigate the lunchroom, the playground, the hallways, and so forth. Copy and distribute the picture dictionaries from this book to aid communication.

Use Student's Native Language

Even if your only Spanish phrase is *Buenos días*, by starting your day with these words, you can immediately connect with your Spanish-speaking students (Flannery, 2006). In fact, one purpose of this book is to give teachers as many of these phrases for quick connection as possible.

Create a Visual Class Schedule

When an ELL student first arrives in your classroom, his or her first priority will be physically getting to the right places at the right times (Weaver, 2005). If you are an elementary school teacher, post a clear and concise daily schedule in your room, using pictures to describe the elements of the day. You might ask the ELL student to help you create this planner. If you are a single-subject teacher, consider creating a high-visual class schedule that ELL students can carry as they navigate their day.

Be Aware of Your Speaking Style

Avoid slang, incorrect usage, and difficult sentence constructions in your own speech. Whenever possible, strive for clear, concise phrases.

Modify Assignments

Your student struggling with language difficulties can be similar to other struggling students. Take care in modifying assignments so that they are not outside the abilities of your ELL students. Consider using hands-on learning, graphic organizers, cooperative learning, and discovery-based activities instead of textbook or lecture-format teaching.

For a more detailed look at instructional strategies for use with ELL students, consult one of the following in-depth guides:

- *Children With Limited English: Teaching Strategies for the Regular Classroom.* Ellen Kottler and Jeffrey A. Kottler. Thousand Oaks, CA: Corwin Press, 2001.
- *Making Content Comprehensible for English Language Learners: The SIOP Model.* Jana Echevarria, MaryEllen Vogt, and Deborah J. Short. Boston: Allyn & Bacon, 2003.
- *Fifty Strategies for Teaching English Language Learners.* Adrienne Harrell and Michael Jordan. Englewood Cliffs, NJ: Prentice Hall, 2003.

WORKING WITH TRANSLATIONS

The certified translation companies ASET Quality Translations and Transperfect Translations both worked to ensure accurate translation of the resources in this book. ASET provided the initial translations and Transperfect checked this work. Both companies have a long history of professional, native-language translators working with Fortune 500 companies, and the authors of this book found both companies to be well informed and experienced throughout the translation process.

However, inherent in this process is the possibility for stylistic differences that create very different translations, all of which are "right." For example, a translation for a first grade class would read quite differently than a translation for a business professional. Thus, especially in the parent letters and reading tests, the goal of translation was not to reproduce the English word for word, but rather to convey the intended message in a culturally appropriate and idiomatic manner. Your students, their families, or bilingual members of your staff might find places in these translations in which the tone or the content are different than the included English. In each case this is a conscious choice on the part of the authors and the translators.

As you will notice, the majority of these languages are written using non-English alphabets. If you are working with ELL students who read in their native languages, you can converse by pointing to the phrases you wish to communicate. If your students do not read in any language, use the included English transliterations and pronunciation guides to make your best attempt at speaking.

However, as you might have guessed, the pronunciation guides will not immediately make you bilingual. This is especially true when working with tonal languages, such as Vietnamese, Cantonese, Navajo, and Hmong, in which slight pitch variations affect meaning. In fact, due to the difficulty of pronouncing tonal languages the authors of this book debated removing the pronunciation guides from these chapters. The rationale for including these resources is twofold—first, in the process of integrating a student into your school community, your attempt at communication using a student's language can be as empowering as your actual success with the language, and second, with your ELL student's help you may, in fact, learn to speak a few of these words or phrases in an intelligible way. Again, this book offers the starting point for basic communication, and even in these tonal languages, this book offers the opportunity to use a combination of speaking, pictures, and gestures to get your point across.

1

Spanish

El saber no ocupa lugar

(One can never know too much)

CULTURAL FACTS

Spanish Speakers in the United States

According to the U.S. Census Bureau's *American Community Survey*, in 2006 there were nearly 36 million foreign-born people of Latino descent living in the United States. This is approximately 12 percent of the country's total population. Of these 36 million, just over half reported speaking English "less than well" (U.S. Census Bureau, 2007). The boom in both legal and illegal immigration have made Latinos the largest minority in the United States, surpassing African Americans. About 60 percent of the Spanish-speaking students in the United States are from Mexico, 15 percent from Puerto Rico, 10 percent from Cuba, another 10 percent from Central and South America, and 5 percent are from other countries. However, your Spanish-speaking students are increasingly likely to have been born stateside (Greenberg, 2001)—and you may notice tension between those students who are recently arrived and those who have been living in the United States for some time. This group of recent arrivals has come to define the ELL (English Language Learner) population in the United States and to guide ELL teaching strategies.

The Spanish Language

Of the ten languages in this book, Spanish is by far the most closely related to English in pronunciation, vocabulary, grammar, and writing system. Spoken by about 350 million people worldwide, Spanish is an official language of the United Nations and is the most common second language throughout the United States. However, it's not safe to assume that the newest non-English-speaking addition to your class, who happens to be from South America, speaks Spanish. Quechua and Portuguese, though phonetically rather similar to Spanish in Anglo ears, are distinct languages, and your well-meaning attempts at Spanish may be as useful as if you were speaking French.

Latino Religion and Culture

The Spanish speakers in your classroom might be as culturally different from one another as Siberia is to Cyprus, which represents the same geographical difference as that between Tijuana, Mexico and Santiago, Chile—nearly 5,500 miles! With this geographic and cultural plurality in mind, it is important to be especially aware of potential stereotyping in the classroom. First explore your students' countries of origin before assuming cultural traditions.

That being said, Catholicism is the dominant religion in the majority of your Latino students' countries of origin. This Mary-centered Catholicism creates instant respect for mothers and other females in authority roles, but lessens the respect given to or earned by female peers who have a less virginal image (Ortiz, 1995).

Latin American Holidays and Other Important Days

February or March: *Carnaval* is a celebration that takes place throughout the Spanish-speaking world before Lent.

March or April: *Semana Santa,* or the holy week of Easter, is the most important Catholic celebration in South America, with processions and prayer marking each day.

May 5: *Cinco de Mayo* commemorates the Mexican victory over the French army in 1862.

November 1: *Día de Todos los Santos,* or All Saints' Day, also known as *Día de los Muertos* (Day of the Dead), is celebrated with food and family in most of the Latin American world.

December 12: *Día de Nuestra Señora de Guadalupe* is a feast honoring Mexico's patron saint.

Pronunciation and Alphabet

Spanish can be pronounced passably using the sounds of the English language, with the following major differences:

- Stress falls on the last or second-to-last syllable unless marked with an accent
- Double r (*rr*) is rolled
- The letter *ñ* takes the place of *ny*, is pronounced like the first *n* in *onion*, and is distinct from the letter *n* alone
- Double l (*ll*) is pronounced like the *y* in *you*
- The letter *j* is pronounced like a guttural *h*
- The letter *x* is usually pronounced like *ks* between vowels and like *s* before a consonant

Communication With Home: Useful Phrases

English	Spanish	Pronunciation Guide
Parents	Los padres	Los **pah**-drays
Mother	La madre	Lah **mah**-dray
Father	El padre	El **pah**-dray
Aunt	La tía	Lah **tee**-ah
Uncle	El tío	El **tee**-oh
Brother	El hermano	El air-**mah**-noh
Sister	La hermana	Lah air-**mah**-nah
Cousin	La prima/El primo	Lah **pree**-mah/El **pree**-moh
Grandfather	El abuelo	El ah-**bway**-loh
Grandmother	La abuela	Lah ah-**bway**-lah
Boyfriend/Girlfriend	El novio/La novia	El **noh**-vyoh/Lah **noh**-vyah
Whom do you live with?	¿Con quién vives?	¿Con kee-**en** **vee**-vays?
What is your phone number?	¿Cuál es tu número de teléfono?	¿Kwal es too **noo**-mair-oh day te-**lay**-foh-noh?
Please show this note to your ____.	Muéstrale esta nota a tu ____.	**Mwes**-trah-lay **ays**-tah **noh**-tah ah too ____.
Please get this signed, and bring it back.	Por favor haz firmar esto, y me lo devuelves.	Por fahv-**or** ahz feer-**mar** **ays**-toh, ee may loh de-**vwel**-ves.
Please have your ____ call me at school.	Dile a tu ____ que me llame a la escuela.	**Dee**-lay ah too ____ kay may **yah**-may ah lah es-**kway**-lah.

Classroom Communication: Useful Phrases

English	Spanish	Pronunciation Guide
Sit down, please.	Siéntate, por favor.	**Syen**-tah-tay, por fah-**vor.**
The assignment is on the board.	La tarea está en la pizarra.	Lah tah-**ray**-ah es-**tah** en lah pee-**zah**-rrah.
Pay attention!	¡Presta atención!	**¡Pres**-tah ah-ten-**syon!**
Good job!	¡Buen trabajo!	¡Bwayn trah-**bah**-hoh!
Excellent!	¡Excelente!	¡Ek-se-**len**-tay!
Do you need help?	¿Necesitas ayuda?	¿Ne-se-**see**-tahs ah-**yoo**-dah?
Do you understand?	¿Entiendes?	¿En-tee-**en**-days?
Do you understand the assignment?	¿Entiendes la tarea?	¿En-tee-**en**-days lah tah-**ray**-ah?
Thanks for listening.	Gracias por escuchar.	**Grah**-syas por es-koo-**char.**
Open your book to page ____.	Abre el libro en la página ____.	**Ah**-bray el **lee**-broh en la **pah**-hee-nah ____.
I know it's hard; do the best you can.	Yo sé que es difícil; haz lo mejor que puedas.	Yo say kay es dee-**fee**-seel; ahz loh may-**hor** kay **pway**-dahs.
How do you say ____ in Spanish?	¿Cómo se dice ____ en español?	**¿Ko**-moh say **dee**-say ____ en es-pah-**nyol?**
What do you think about ____?	¿Qué piensas de ____?	¿Kay pee-**en**-sahs day ____?
I would like you to ____.	Quisiera que tú ____.	Kee-**syair**-ah kay too ____.
Do you know how to ____?	¿Sabes como ____?	**¿Sah**-bays **koh**-moh ____?
Is this easy or hard?	¿Es fácil o difícil?	¿Es **fah**-seel oh dee-**fee**-ceel?
Quiet, please.	Silencio, por favor.	See-**len**-syoh, por fah-**vor.**
Please be careful.	Ten cuidado, por favor.	Ten kwee-**dah**-doh, por fah-**vor.**

Student Communication: Useful Phrases

English	Spanish	Pronunciation Guide
I am new.	Soy nuevo.	Soy **nway**-voh.
I don't speak English.	No hablo ingles.	No **ah**-bloh een-**glays.**
Do you speak Spanish?	¿Hablas español?	¿**Ah**-blas es-pah-**nyol**?
I'm from ____.	Soy de ____.	Soy day ____.
I'm sorry.	Lo siento.	Loh **syen**-toh.
Excuse me.	Perdón.	Pair-**dohn.**
Thanks.	Gracias.	Grah-syas.
My name is ____.	Me llamo ____.	May yah-moh ____.
Can you help me?	¿Puedes ayudarme?	¿Pway-days ah-yoo-dar-may?
Where is the ____?	¿Dónde está el/la ____?	¿Dohn-day es-tah el/lah ____?
Can I play?	¿Puedo jugar?	¿Pway-doh hoo-gar?

Classroom Supplies: Class Dictionary

Book	Computer	Crayons	Eraser
El libro	La computadora	Los crayones	La goma
el **lee**-broh	lah com-poo-tah-**doh**-rah	lohs cray-**ohn**-ays	lah **goh**-mah
Folder	Glue	Markers	Note
La carpeta	El pegamento	Los marcadores	La nota
lah car-pay-tah	el pay-gah-**mayn**-toh	lohs mar-cah-**doh**-rays	lah **noh**-tah
Notebook	Paint	Paperclip	Pen
El cuaderno	La pintura	El clip	La pluma
el kwah-**dayr**-noh	lah peen-**too**-rah	el kleep	lah **ploo**-mah
Pencil	Piece of Paper	Poster	Printer
El lápiz	Una hoja de papel	El cartel	La impresora
el **lah**-pees	**oon**-ah **oh**-ha day pah-**pel**	el kar-**tel**	lah eem-pray-**so**-rah
Ruler	Scissors	Stapler	Tape
La regla	Las tijeras	La grapadora	La cinta
lah **ray**-glah	lahs tee-**hair**-ahs	lah grah-pah-**doh**-rah	lah **seen**-tah

School Mechanics: Class Dictionary

Absent	Bathroom	Bell	Cafeteria
Ausente	El baño	El timbre	La cafetería
ow-**sen**-tay	el **bah**-nyoh	el **teem**-bray	lah cah-fay-tair-**ee**-ah
Class Period	**Clock**	**Counselor**	**To Get a Drink**
La hora de clase	El reloj	El consejero/La consejera	Beber algo
lah **oh**-rah day **clah**-say	el ray-**loh**	el kohn-say-**hair**-oh/la kohn-say-**hair**-ah	bay-**bair ahl**-goh
Gymnasium	**Library**	**Locker**	**Lunch**
El gimnasio	La biblioteca	El armario	El almuerzo
el heem-**nah**-syoh	lah bee-blyoh-**tay**-kah	el ahr-**mah**-ryoh	el ahl-**mwair**-zoh
Office	**Playground**	**Principal**	**Recess**
La oficina	El patio de recreo	El director/La directora	El recreo
lah oh-fee-**see**-nah	**pah**-tyoh day ray-**cray**-oh	el dee-rek-**tor**/lah dee-rek-**tor**-a	el ray-**cray**-oh
Schedule	**Secretary**	**Tardy**	**Teacher**
El horario	El secretario/La secretaria	Tarde	El maestro/La maestra
el oh-**rah**-ryoh	el say-cray-**tah**-ryoh/la say-cray-**tah**-ryah	**tar**-day	el mah-**ays**-troh/lah mah-**ays**-trah

Schedule table inset:

8:30	Welcome/Class Business
9:00	Language Arts
10:30	Mathematics
11:30	Social Studies
12:00	Lunch
1:00	Science
2:00	Art/Music/PE

Assignment Words: Class Dictionary

Assignment	Correct	Design	Directions
Los trabajos	Correcto	El diseño	Las instrucciones
lohs trah-**bah**-hohs	koh-**rrek**-toh	el dee-**say**-nyoh	lahs eens-trook-**syon**-ays
To Discuss	**To Draw**	**Due Date**	**Grade**
Hablar de	Dibujar	La fecha límite	La nota
ah-**blar** day	dee-boo-**har**	lah **fay**-cha **lee**-mee-tay	lah **no**-tah
To Help	**Homework**	**To Listen**	**Permission Letter**
Ayudar	La tarea	Escuchar	La carta de permiso
ah-yoo-**dar**	lah tah-**ray**-ah	es-koo-**char**	lah **kar**-tah day pair-**mee**-soh
Questions	**To Read**	**Stop**	**To Take Notes**
Las preguntas	Leer	Alto	Tomar apuntes
las pray-**goon**-tahs	lay-**air**	**ahl**-toh	toh-**mar** ah-**poon**-tays
Test	**To Turn In**	**To Write**	**Wrong**
El examen	Entregar	Escribir	Equivocado
el ay-**ksah**-men	en-tray-**gar**	es-cree-**beer**	ay-kee-voh-**kah**-doh

Playground and Physical Education Vocabulary: Class Dictionary

Ball	Baseball	Basketball	To Catch
La pelota lah pay-**loh**-tah	El béisbol el **bayees**-bohl	El baloncesto el bah-lohn-**says**-toh	Atrapar ah-trah-**par**
To Change	Circle	Drill	Field
Cambiar kahm-**byar**	El círculo el **seer**-koo-loh	Un ejercicio oon ay-hair-**see**-syoh	El campo el **kahm**-poh
To Follow	Football (American)	Four Square	Go in Front
Seguir say-**geer**	El fútbol americano el **foot**-bohl ah- mair-ee-**cah**-noh	Four square four square	Va al frente vah ahl **frehn**-tay
Gym Clothes	Handball	To Hit	Hurt
El uniforme para la clase de educación física el oon-ee-**for**-may **pah**-rah lah **clah**-say day eh-doo-kah-**syon** **fee**-see-kah	Balon mano bah-**lohn mah**-noh	Golpear gol-pay-**ar**	Herido/Herida air-**ee**-doh/air-**ee**-dah
To Jump	Jumprope	Kickball	Line
Saltar sahl-**tar**	Saltar la cuerda sahl-**tar** lah **kwair**-dah	Kickball kickball	La fila/La cola lah **fee**-lah/lah **koh**-lah

Lock	**Locker Room**	**To Lose**	**Out of Bounds**
La cerradura	El vestuario	Perder	Fuera de juego
lah sairr-ah-**doo**-rah	el ves-**twah**-ryoh	pair-**dair**	**fwair**-ah day **hway**-goh
To Run	**The Rules**	**Shoes**	**Sideline**
Correr	Las reglas	Los zapatos	La línea lateral
koh-**rrair**	lahs **ray**-glahs	lohs sah-**pah**-tohs	lah **lee**-nya lah-tair-**ahl**
Soccer	**Sport**	**To Stretch**	**Team**
El fútbol	Los deportes	Estirarse	El equipo
el **foot**-bohl	lohs day-**por**-tays	ays-tee-**rahr**-say	el ay-**kee**-poh
Tetherball	**To Throw**	**Volleyball**	**Whistle**
Tetherball	Tirar	El voleibol	El silbato
tetherball	tee-**rahr**	el voh-**lay**-bohl	el seel-**bah**-toh

Science Vocabulary: Class Dictionary

Acid	Animal	Base	Climate
El ácido	El animal	La base	El clima
el **ah**-see-doh	el ah-nee-**mahl**	lah **bah**-say	el **klee**-mah
Dinosaur	**Earth**	**Electricity**	**Energy**
El dinosaurio	Tierra	Electricidad	La energía
el dee-no-**sow**-ryo	tee-**airr**-ah	ay-lek-tree-see-**dahd**	lah ay-nair-**hee**-ah
Environment	**Experiment**	**Extinct**	**Hypothesis**
El medio ambiente	El experimento	Extinto	La hipótesis
el **may**-dyoh ahm-**byehn**-tay	el es-pair-ee-**mehn**-toh	es-**teen**-toh	lah ee-**poh**-tay-cease
To Investigate	**Lab Notebook**	**Laboratory**	**Matter**
	El cuaderno de laboratorio		
Investigar	el kwah-**dair**-noh day	El laboratorio	Sustancia
een-ves-tee-**gar**	lah-boh-rah-**toh**-ryoh	el lah-boh-rah-**toh**-ryoh	soos-**tahn**-syah
Motion	**Planet**	**Plant**	**Science**
Movimiento	El planeta	La planta	Las ciencias
moh-vee-**myen**-toh	el plah-**nay**-tah	lah **plahn**-tah	lahs **syehn**-syahs

Math Vocabulary: Class Dictionary

To Add **+** Sumar soo-**mar**	Answer $1 + 1 = ②$ La respuesta lah rehs-**pways**-tah	To Calculate $\begin{array}{r} 7 \\ 8 \\ +5 \\ \hline 20 \end{array}$ Calcular kal-koo-**lar**	Calculator La calculadora lah kal-koo-lah-**doh**-rah
To Combine Combinar kohm-bee-**nar**	To Divide ÷ Dividir dee-vee-**deer**	Equation $2 + 3 = 5$ La ecuación lah eh-kwah-**syohn**	Exponent A^4 El exponente el es-poh-**nehn**-teh
Graph La gráfica lah **grah**-fee-kah	Math Las matemáticas lahs mah-tay-**mah**-tee-kahs	To Multiply $3 ⊗ 2$ Multiplicar mool-tee-plee-**kar**	Numbers 1 2 3 4 5 6 7 8 9 Los números lohs **noo**-meh-rohs
To Order 1, 2, 3, 4 Ordenar or-deh-**nar**	Problem $1 + 3 = ?$ El problema el proh-**blay**-mah	Property $x(y + 2)$ La propiedad lah proh-pyeh-**dahd**	To Prove Probar proh-**bar**
To Simplify $\frac{3X + 42}{4} = 6X \longrightarrow X = 2$ Simplificar seem-plee-fee-**kar**	To Solve $3x = 12$ $X = 4$ Solucionar soh-loo-syoh-**nar**	To Subtract $12 ⊖ 6$ Restar rehs-**tar**	Variable x, y La variable lah vah-**rya**-blay

Social Studies Vocabulary: Class Dictionary

Africa África **ah**-free-kah	Asia Asia **ah**-sya	Australia Australia ow-**strah**-lyah	Buddhist Budista boo-**dees**-tah
Christian Cristiano/Cristiana krees-**tyah**-noh/ krees-**tyah**-nah	Citizenship Ciudadanía syoo-dah-dah-**nee**-ah	Continent El continente el kohn-tee-**nen**-teh	Country El país el pah-**ees**
Democracy Democracia deh-moh-**krah**-syah	Europe Europa ay-oo-**roh**-pah	Geography La geografía lah hay-oh-grah-**fee**-ah	Government Gobierno el goh-**byair**-noh
Hinduism Hinduísmo een-doo-**ees**-moh	History La historia lah ees-**toh**-rya	Jewish Judío/Judía hoo-**dee**-oh/hoo-**dee**-ah	Map El mapa el **mah**-pah
Muslim Musulmán/Musulmána moo-sool-**mahn**/moo- sool-**mahn**-ah	North American Norteamericano/ Norteamericana nor-tay-ah-mair-ee-**kah**-noh/ nor-tay-ah-mair-ee-**kah**-nah	South America Sudamérica soo-dah-**mair**-ee-kah	World El mundo el **moon**-doh

Welcome to My Classroom

Dear Parent or Guardian,

I would like to welcome your child to my classroom. The first couple of weeks can be difficult for students who don't yet speak English, but by working with you as a team I hope to make the transition as smooth as possible. While my Spanish is not strong, I will do the best I can to communicate what is expected of your child in the classroom and in the school. Please feel free to stop by before or just after school, or to call anytime.

Again, welcome to our school! I look forward to speaking with you soon.

Sincerely,

Estimados Padres o Tutores:

Ante todo le quiero dar una bienvenida a su hijo(a) a mi aula. Les quiero decir que las primeras semanas pueden ser difíciles para los alumnos que todavía no hablan inglés, pero si trabajamos juntos como equipo podemos lograr que la transición sea lo más fácil y agradable posible. Si bien mi español no es perfecto, haré lo mejor que pueda para comunicarme con su hijo(a) en cuanto a lo que se espera de él o ella en el aula y en la escuela en general. No duden en visitarme antes o después de las clases o en llamarme en cualquier momento.

¡Otra vez, bienvenidos a nuestra escuela! Espero hablar con ustedes pronto.

Les saluda atentamente,

Your Child Is a Pleasure to Have in Class

Dear Parent or Guardian,

This is a note of thanks to let you know that your child is a pleasure to have in class and to thank you for the work you do at home to help your child succeed. Though your child sometimes has difficulties with the language, he or she is trying hard and making progress every day. Keep up the good work!

Sincerely,

Estimados Padres o Tutores:

Esta es una nota de agradecimiento para informarles que es un placer tener a su hijo(a) en mi clase y para agradecerles todo lo que hacen en casa para apoyar sus esfuerzos. Aunque su hijo(a) a veces tiene dificultades con el idioma, él/ella está trabajando mucho y cada día veo más progreso. ¡Sigan así!

Les saluda atentamente,

Your Child Is Not Performing Up to Ability

Dear Parent or Guardian,

Though your child is smart and capable, he or she is not performing up to his or her ability. We understand that it's difficult to learn when you don't speak the language, but the only way to learn is to try, and your child needs to try harder. If you have any questions, please stop by before or just after school, or give me a call anytime.

Sincerely,

Estimados Padres o Tutores:

Aunque su hijo(a) tiene la capacidad y la inteligencia necesarias, no está haciendo todo lo que puede para aprender. Entendemos que es difícil aprender cuando no se habla bien el idioma, pero la única manera de aprender es esforzarse y su hijo necesita poner más esfuerzo. Si tienen cualquier pregunta, no duden en visitarme antes o después de clases o llamarme por teléfono en cualquier momento.

Les saluda atentamente,

Please Schedule a Meeting

Dear Parent or Guardian,

Please call or stop by the school office to schedule a meeting concerning your child. We understand that your time is valuable, but this is very important.

Sincerely,

Estimados Padres o Tutores:

Les ruego que me llamen o vengan a la oficina de la escuela para hacer una cita con respecto a su hijo(a). Entendemos que su tiempo es valioso, pero esto es muy importante. Gracias de antemano.

Les saluda atentamente,

I am the parent of _____.

Soy el padre de _____.

❑   I need a translator.

❑   Necesito un traductor.

Your Child's Behavior Is a Problem

Dear Parent or Guardian,

Your child's behavior is unacceptable. Not only does your child create an environment where he or she cannot learn, but your child is also disrupting the learning of others. I hope we can work as a team to help your child learn to behave appropriately in school. If your child continues his or her current behavior, it will result in severe disciplinary action. If you have any questions, please stop by before or just after school, or give me a call anytime.

Sincerely,

Estimados Padres o Tutores:

La conducta de su hijo(a) es inaceptable. No solamente está creando un ambiente que trastorna su aprendizaje, sino que también está trastornando el aprendizaje de los demás en la clase. Espero que podamos trabajar en equipo para remediar esta situación. Si su hijo(a) continúa con su conducta actual, tendrá como resultado medidas disciplinarias severas. Si tienen cualquier preguntas, no duden en visitarme antes o después de clases o de llamarme en cualquier momento.

Les saluda atentamente,

Absences Are Hurting Performance

Dear Parent or Guardian,

Your child's absences are hurting his or her performance. Much of what we do in school builds on what we did the day before; if a student is absent it can be very hard to catch up. I hope that we can work together as a team to help make sure that your child attends class. If you have any questions, please stop by before or just after school, or give me a call anytime.

Sincerely,

Estimados Padres o Tutores:

Las ausencias de su hijo(a) están afectando su rendimiento. Mucho de lo que hacemos en clase se relaciona con lo que se vio el día anterior; así que si un estudiante se ausenta, es probable que vaya a tener muchas dificultades después. Espero que podamos trabajar juntos como equipo para asegurarnos de que su hijo(a) asista a clases. Si tienen preguntas, no duden en visitarme antes o después de clases o de llamarme en cualquier momento.

Les saluda atentamente,

Tardiness Is Hurting Performance

Dear Parent or Guardian,

Your child is frequently late to class, and this tardiness is hurting his or her performance. By missing the beginning of the period, your child misses important directions and information, making it impossible for him or her to keep up with the rest of the class. I hope that we can work together as a team to help make sure that your child attends class. If you have any questions, please stop by before or just after school, or give me a call anytime.

Sincerely,

Estimados Padres o Tutores:

Su hijo(a) ha llegado con frecuencia tarde a clase, y esto está afectando su rendimiento. Si no entra al principio de la clase, no recibe las instrucciones e información importantes, con lo que es imposible que mantenga el mismo ritmo que los demás. Si tienen preguntas, no duden en visitarme antes o después de clases o de llamarme en cualquier momento.

Les saluda atentamente,

General Resources That School Offers

Dear Parent or Guardian,

The teachers and staff here at school hope to help you and your child in any way we can. The school offers translators and may also be able to help with school supplies and other services. Please feel free to stop by the school office anytime to explore the services available. If you work during the day, you can always call or send a note with your child. We hope to talk to you soon!

Sincerely,

Estimados Padres o Tutores:

Los maestros y el personal de la escuela esperamos poder ayudarle a usted y a su hijo(a) en cualquier manera que podamos. La escuela le ofrece traductores y también puede ayudar a conseguir materiales de clase y otros servicios. Si tienen cualquier pregunta no duden en visitarme en cualquier momento para consultar los servicios disponibles. Si trabajan durante el día, pueden llamarme o mandarme una nota con su hijo.

¡Esperamos hablar con ustedes pronto!

Les saluda atentamente,

2

Vietnamese

Mot mieng khi doi bang mot goi khi no

(A small piece of food while starving is better than a feast while full)

CULTURAL FACTS

Vietnamese in the United States

There have been three waves of Vietnamese immigration to the United States, and each has faced unique assimilation challenges. The first wave, in 1975, directly followed the Vietnam War as many educated and affluent Vietnamese fled the new communist regime. Immigrants of the first wave frequently found themselves working and living below the standards they knew in Vietnam. The next wave of refugees, known as "boat people," risked their lives in the late 1970s and through the 1980s to escape Vietnam by any means possible. This wave benefited both from the experience and infrastructure established by the first Vietnamese immigrants, and from the increased, rather than decreased, opportunities they found in the United States relative to what they were used to. The third wave of Vietnamese immigration, in the 1990s, was a result of an agreement between the United States and Vietnam to bring to the United States former soldiers of the South Vietnamese army, most of whom had been imprisoned in communist camps. Like the first wave of immigrants, this third wave was composed primarily of skilled workers who found their opportunities in the United States limited in comparison with what they had left behind.

The Vietnamese Language

The Vietnamese language is a combination of Mon-Khmer, Thai, and Chinese. While there are three main dialects (northern, central, and southern), they are mutually intelligible and differ mostly in pronunciation and in the use of a few dialect-specific phrases. For example, a Saigon *q* is like an English *w,* while a Hanoi *q* sounds as it would in English. There are over eighty million speakers of Vietnamese, located primarily in Vietnam, the United States, Cambodia, China, and France.

Vietnamese Religion and Culture

In Vietnam, family is very important. Traditionally, a married couple will live with and care for the husband's parents. Thus it is very important for a couple to have at least one son. While the people of Vietnam are traditionally Confucian or Mahayana Buddhist, the 1999 census found that 80 percent of Vietnamese did not consider themselves religious. Many of the religious 20 percent were followers of the so-called *Tam Giáo* ("triple religion"), which mixes Zen-tinged Mahayana Buddhism with Confucianism and Taoism. The largest minority religions are Roman Catholic, Hoa Hao, and Protestant, with the largest Protestant churches being the Evangelical Church of Vietnam and the Montagnard Evangelical Church. Vietnam has a rich history of art and architecture, with much of the latter influenced by Chinese and French styles.

Vietnamese Holidays and Other Important Days

The Vietnamese holidays follow the lunar calendar. Search "Vietnam Festival Calendar" online for the current year's dates.

Tet Nguyen Dan: The celebration of the lunar new year is held sometime in late January or early February.

Tet Khai Ha: Everyone celebrates the coming of spring.

Tet Han Thuc: People offer deceased ancestors cold food on the third day of the third lunar month.

Tet Doan Ngo: This holiday is known as "exterminating harmful insects," a time for cleansing.

Tet Trung Thu: This midautumn festival is held in September.

Tet Ha Nguyen: The new rice festival is celebrated on the first day of the tenth lunar month.

Tet Tao Quan: The festival of household gods heralds the end of the year and the coming of *Tet Nguyen Dan.*

Pronunciation and Alphabet

Vietnamese is written using an alphabet called *Quõn Ngu,* which adds diacritics to the Latin alphabet to indicate tones. There are six tones—no tone, raising, falling, questioning, falling-raising, and weighing—and each tone can indicate a different meaning. Vietnamese is like Hmong in using a Latin alphabet marked for tone, though most Westerners have *less* difficulty with Vietnamese than with Hmong. In addition to the tones, keep the following differences in mind:

ph is like English *f*

t at the beginning of words is like English *d*

th at the beginning of words is like English *t*

x is like English *s*

c is like English *k*

tr is like English *ch* with the tongue tip curled backwards

Communication With Home: Useful Phrases

English	Vietnamese	Pronunciation Guide
Parents	*Phụ huynh*	Fu hu-wing
Mother	*Mẹ*	Me
Father	*Cha*	Cha
Aunt	*Cô/Dì*	C-O/Yee
Uncle	*Cậu/Chú/Bác*	Cauw/Choo/Back
Brother	*Anh/Em*	A-ine/Em
Sister	*Chị/Em*	Chee/Em
Cousin	*Anh/Chị/Em họ*	Ayn/Chee/Em haw
Boyfriend/Girlfriend	*Bạn trai/Bạn gái*	Ban ch-y/Ban g-eye
Whom do you live with?	*Em sống với ai?*	Em sa-own-ng v-ay eye?
What is your phone number?	*Số điện thoại của em là số mấy?*	Sew din t-hoy ko-ore em la sew m-ay?
Please show this note to your ____.	*Đưa thông báo này cho ____.*	D-yur t-h-owng b-ow n-eye ch-aw ____.
Please get this signed and bring it back.	*Đưa giấy này cho gia đình ký tên vào và đem trả lại.*	D-yur xay n-eye ch-aw za d-ing key tain vow va dem cha lie.
Please have your ____ call me at school.	*Nói với ____ gọi điện thoại cho tôi ở trường.*	N-oy v-uh-oy ____ g-oy d-in ch-aw t-O-y uh ch-ua-ung.

Classroom Communication: Useful Phrases

English	Vietnamese	Pronunciation Guide
Sit down please.	*Ngồi xuống nào.*	Ng-O-y s-ua-ung now.
The assignment is on the board.	*Bài tập ghi trên bảng.*	B-eye tup g-ee chain b-aeng.
Pay attention!	*Chú ý đây!*	Choo eee d-ay!
Good job.	*Làm tốt lắm.*	Lamb t-O-t lam.
Excellent!	*Xuất sắc!*	S-oo-ut s-aac!
Do you need help?	*Em có cần giúp gì không?*	Em caw cun zoop k-h-Own?
Do you understand?	*Em có hiểu không?*	Em caw hugh k-h-Own?
Do you understand the assignment?	*Em có hiểu bài tập không?*	Em caw hugh b-eye tup k-h-Own?
Thanks for listening.	*Cám ơn các em đã nghe.*	Cam un cack em da-ah ng-h-e.
Open your book to page ____.	*Mở sách của các em ở trang ____.*	Muh-uh sack ko-ore cac em uh chang ____.
I know it's hard; do the best you can.	*Tôi biết bài này khó; hãy cố gắng nhé.*	T-oy bit b-eye n-eye k-h-aw; ha-eye c-O gu-Aing nh-e.
How do you say ____ in Vietnamese?	*Em nói ____ như thế nào bằng tiếng Việt?*	Em n-oy ____ nh-oo-oi t-h-Ae n-ow ba-ung?
What do you think about ____?	*Em nghĩ gì về ____?*	Em ng-ee-ee zee v-Ae ____?
I would like you to ____.	*Tôi muốn em ____.*	T-oy moo-Own em ____.
Do you know how to ____?	*Em có biết cách ____?*	Em c-aw bit k-eye-t ____?
Is this easy or hard?	*Bài này dễ hay khó?*	B-eye n-eye yay-A h-eye k-h-aw?
Quiet, please.	*Xin im lặng.*	Seen eem l-awn.
Please be careful.	*Hãy cẩn thận.*	H-ay c-un t-hun.

Student Communication: Useful Phrases

English	Vietnamese	Pronunciation Guide
I am new.	*Em là người mới đến.*	Em l-ah ng-u-oy m-uh-oi dane.
I don't speak English.	*Em không nói được tiếng Anh.*	Em k-h-own-ng n-oy d-uh-ork t-i-ang A-ine.
Do you speak ____?	*Em nói tiếng ____?*	Em n-oy t-i-ang ____?
I'm from ____.	*Em đến từ ____.*	Em d-ane t-oo-uh ____.
I'm sorry.	*Em rất tiếc.*	Em r-ut t-ierck.
Excuse me.	*Em xin lỗi.*	Em seen l-o-oi.
Thanks.	*Cám ơn.*	C-am un.
My name is ____.	*Tên em là ____.*	Tain em l-uh ____.
Can you help me?	*Thầy/Cô có thể giúp em không?*	T-h-ay/c-oh c-aw t-h-ae z-oop em k-h-own-ng?
Where is the ____?	*____ nằm ở đâu?*	____ n-u-em uh d-uh-ow?
Can I play?	*Em có thể chơi không?*	Em c-aw t-h-a-ay ch-uh-uh k-h-own-ng?

Classroom Supplies: Class Dictionary

Book	Computer	Crayons	Eraser
Sách	*Máy điện toán*	*Phấn mều*	*Cục gôm*
s-ack	m-eye din t-uoan	fan mau	c-ook g-ome
Folder	Glue	Markers	Note
Bìa cứng	*Keo ẩn*	*Bút vẽ*	*Ghi chú*
b-ear c-oong	keo gian	b-oot ve-air	g-ee choo
Notebook	Paint	Paperclip	Pen
Tập làm bài	*Vẽ*	*Kẹp giấy*	*Viết mực*
tup lamb b-eye	ve-eh	kep za-ay	v-it ma-uc
Pencil	Piece of Paper	Poster	Printer
Viết chì	*Tờ giấy*	*Áp-phích*	*Máy in*
v-it ch-ee	tuh za-ay	up-fic	my-ai een
Ruler	Scissors	Stapler	Tape
Cây thước	*Cái kéo*	*Đồ bấm giấy*	*Dy buộc*
c-ay t-h-ork	c-eye k-e-eo	doe bum za-ay	giei buot

School Mechanics: Class Dictionary

Absent	Bathroom	Bell	Cafeteria
Vắng mặt	*Phòng vệ sinh*	*Chuông*	*Phòng ăn*
v-u-ang mite	fong v-ae sing	chu-own-ng	fong a-ine
Class Period	Clock	Counselor	To Get a Drink
Giờ học	*Đồng hồ*	*Cố vấn*	*Để đi uống nước*
zuh h-aw-k	d-own-ng h-oh	c-oh-oh vun	d-a-ay oo-wong n-u-ork
Gymnasium	Library	Locker	Lunch
Phòng tập	*Thư viện*	*Tủ khóa*	*Bữa ăn trưa*
f-aw-ong tup	t-h-uu vin	t-oo-oo k-h-wa	b-u-a a-in ch-u-a
Office	Playground	Principal	Recess
Văn phòng	*Sn chơi*	*Hiệu trưởng*	*Giờ ra chơi*
v-a-ine fong	san choi	h-ew ch-u-ang	zuh ra ch-uh-uh
Schedule	Secretary	Tardy	Teacher
Thời khóa biểu	*Thư ký*	*Trễ học*	*Giáo viên*
t-h-uh k-h-w-ah b-ew	t-h-uu k-ee	ch-a-ay h-aw-k	Z-ow vin

Schedule cell contents:

8:30	Welcome/Class Business
9:00	Language Arts
10:30	Mathematics
11:30	Social Studies
12:00	Lunch
1:00	Science
2:00	Art/Music/PE

Assignment Words: Class Dictionary

Assignment	Correct	Design	Directions
Bài tập b-eye tup	*Đúng* d-oong	*Phác thảo* f-ack t-h-ow	*Chỉ dẫn* ch-ee-ee y-un
To Discuss	To Draw	Due Date	Grade
Để thảo luận d-a-ay t-h-ow l-u-on	*Để vẽ* d-a-ay ve-eh	*Ngày đáo hạn* ng-eye y-ow han	*Điểm* d-i-im
To Help	Homework	To Listen	Permission Letter
Để giúp đỡ d-a-ay z-oop d-uh-uh	*Bài tập về nhà làm* b-eye tup v-a n-h-ah l-ah-m	*Để nghe* d-a-ay ng-eh	*Thư cho phép* t-h-uu ch-aw fep
Questions	To Read	Stop	To Take Notes
Câu hỏi c-a-ow h-oy	*Để đọc* d-a-ay dock	*Dừng lại* y-ung l-eye	*Để ghi chú* d-a-ay g-ee choo
Test	To Turn In	To Write	Wrong
Bài kiểm tra b-eye k-i-im cha	*Để nộp bài* d-a-ay nope b-eye	*Để viết* d-a-ay vit	*Sai* s-eye

Playground and Physical Education Vocabulary: Class Dictionary

Ball	Baseball	Basketball	To Catch
Trái bóng ch-eye b-aw-ong	*Bóng chày* b-awng ch-eye	*Bóng rỗ* b-awng r-o	*Để chụp* d-a-ay ch-oop
To Change	Circle	Drill	Field
Để thay đồ d-a-ay t-h-eye d-oh	*Hình tròn* hing ch-on	*Tập dợt* t-up d-ut	*Sân* s-un
To Follow	Football (American)	Four Square	Go in Front
Để theo sau d-a-ay t-h-ew s-ow	*Đá banh cà na* da-ah b-ine c-ah n-ah	*Trị chơi bĩng bốn ngươi* tro choi bon bon nguoi	*Ln phía trược* len fia truok
Gym Clothes	Handball	To Hit	Hurt
Đồ thể dục d-oh t-h-ae y-ook	*Banh ấm* baen nem	*Để Đánh banh* d-a-ay d-a-ine b-a-ine	*Làm đau/Bị đau* l-a-em d-ow/b-ee d-ow
To Jump	Jumprope	Kickball	Line
Để nhảy d-a-ay n-uh-eye	*Dy để nhảy* giei de nhei	*Banh ả* baen da	*Hàng* h-uh- ang

Lock	Locker Room	To Lose	Out of Bounds
Khóa	*Phòng khóa*	*Để thua*	*Ra khỏi đường ranh giới*
k-h-uh-oa	fong k-h-uh-oa	d-a-ay t-h-uh-ur	ra k-h-uh-oi d-uh-ung r-ine z-uh-oi
The Rules	To Run	Shoes	Sideline
Điều lệ	*Để chạy*	*Giày*	*Đường biên*
d-ew l-ae	d-a-ay ch-eye	z-uh-ay	d-uh-ung b-in
Soccer	Sport	To Stretch	Team
Bóng đá	*Thể thao*	*Để thư giản*	*Đội*
b-awng d-ah	t-h-a-ay t-h-ow	d-a-ay t-h-ah-ah l-ow-ong	d-oh-oi
Tetherball	To Throw	Volleyball	Whistle
Banh buộc	*Để ném*	*Bóng chuyền*	*Còi*
baen buot	d-a-ay n-em	b-awng ch-u-in	c-aw-oi

Science Vocabulary: Class Dictionary

Acid *Axít* a-xit	Animal *Động vật* d-own-ng vut	Base *Bazơ* ba-zuh	Climate *Khí hậu* k-h-ee h-u-ow
Dinosaur *Khủng long* k-h-oo-ung l-ow-ng	Earth *Trái đất* trai dat	Electricity *điện* dien	Energy *Năng lượng* n-u-ang l-u-uong
Environment *Môi trường* m-o-oi ch-u-uong	Experiment *Thí nghiệm* t-h-ee ng-im	Extinct *Tuyệt chủng* t-oo-it ch-oo-ung	Hypothesis *Giả thuyết* za-ah t-h-oo-et
To Investigate *điệu tra* dieu tra	Lab Notebook *Tập ghi chú phòng thí nghiệm* tup g-ee ch-oo fong t-h-ee ng-im	Laboratory *Phòng thí nghiệm* fong t-h-ee ng-im	Matter *Vấn đề* van de
Motion *Chuyển động* chooin doon	Planet *Hành tinh* hi-an t-ing	Plant *Cây* c-ay	Science *Khoa học* k-h-ore h-ow-ck

Math Vocabulary: Class Dictionary

To Add	Answer	To Calculate	Calculator
+	$1 + 1 = ②$	$\begin{array}{r}7\\8\\+5\\\hline 20\end{array}$	
Để thêm	*Trả lời*	*Để tính toán*	*Máy tính*
d-a-ay t-h-aim	cha-ah l-uh-uh	d-a-ay ting t-oo-oan	m-eye t-i-ing

To Combine	To Divide	Equation	Exponent
	$\div$	$2 + 3 = 5$	A^4
Để kết hợp	*Để chia*	*Phương trình*	*Lũy thừa*
d-a-ay ket hup	d-a-ay ch-i-uh	f-ua-ung ching	l-oo-we t-h-u-uh

Graph	Math	To Multiply	Numbers
		$3 \otimes 2$	$\begin{array}{l}1\ 2\ 3\ 4\ 5\\6\ 7\ 8\ 9\end{array}$
Đồ thị	*Toán*	*Để nhân*	*Con số*
d-oh t-h-ee	t-oo-oan	d-a-ay n-h-un	con s-oh

To Order	Problem	Property	To Prove
$1, 2, 3, 4$	$\begin{array}{l}3x=12\\X=4\end{array}$	$x(y + 2)$	
Để sắp xếp	*Toán đố*	*Tính chất*	*Để chứng minh*
d-a-ay s-uh-ap sape	t-oo-oan d-oh	t-ing chut	d-a-ay ch-uh-ung ming

To Simplify	To Solve	To Subtract	Variable
$\frac{3X + 42}{4} = 6X \longrightarrow X = 2$	$1 + 3 = ?$	$12 \ominus 6$	x, y
Để đơn giản	*Để giải*	*Để trừ*	*Biến thiên*
d-a-ay dun z-ah-un	d-a-ay z-ah-eye	d-a-ay ch-oo	b-i-inn t-h-inn

Social Studies Vocabulary: Class Dictionary

Africa *Phi Châu* fee ch-uh-ow	Asia *Á Châu* ah-ah ch-uh-ow	Australia *Nước c* nu-t uk	Buddhist *Đạo Phật* d-ow f-ut
Christian *Thiên Chúa Giáo* c-oh-ng z-ow	Citizenship *Quyền cơng ân* quuen koong dan	Continent *Lục địa* l-ook d-i	Country *Quốc gia* q-uh-ork za
Democracy *Dn chư* gian chu	Europe *Âu Châu* au ch-uh-ow	Geography *Địa lý* d-i-ah lee	Government *Chính phư* chinh fu
Hinduism *ẤnĐộgío* an doo giao	History *Lịch sử* l-ick s-uh-oo	Jewish *Do Thái* d-aw t-h-eye	Map *Bản đồ* b-ah-an d-oh
Muslim *Hồi giáo* h-oh-oi z-ow	North American *Bắc Mỹ* back m-ee-ee	South America *Nam Mỹ* nam m-ee-ee	World *Thế giới* t-h-ae z-uh-uh

Welcome to My Classroom

Dear Parent or Guardian,

I would like to welcome your child to my classroom. The first couple of weeks can be difficult for students who don't yet speak English, but by working with you as a team I hope to make the transition as smooth as possible. While my Vietnamese is not strong, I will do the best I can to communicate what is expected of your child in the classroom and in the school. Please feel free to stop by before or just after school, or to call anytime.

Again, welcome to our school! I look forward to speaking with you soon.

Sincerely,

Kính gởi Quý Phụ Huynh hay Người Giám Hộ,

Tôi xin chào mừng con của quý vị vào học lớp này. Đối với những học sinh không nói tiếng Anh thì các tuần đầu tiên sẽ khó khăn, nhưng tôi hy vọng mọi việc sẽ trôi chảy khi chúng ta cùng nhau hợp tác. Tôi không nói được tiếng Việt nhiều nhưng sẽ cố gắng hết mức để truyền đạt những đòi hỏi của trường đến con của quý vị trong lớp vàở trường. Xin đừng ngần ngại ghé vào trước hoặc sau giờ học, hay gọi cho tôi bất cứ lúc nào.

Một lần nữa, xin chào mừng tất cả đến trường chúng tôi! Tôi rất mong sớm được nói chuyện với quý vị.

Trân trọng,

Your Child Is a Pleasure to Have in Class

Dear Parent or Guardian,

This is a note of thanks to let you know that your child is a pleasure to have in class and to thank you for the work you do at home to help your child succeed. Though your child sometimes has difficulties with the language, he or she is trying hard and making progress every day. Keep up the good work!

Sincerely,

Kính gởi Quý Phụ Huynh hay Người Giám Hộ,

Đây là thư cám ơn để báo cho quý vị biết rằng chúng tôi rất vui khi có con của quý vị vào học ở lớp này. Dù thỉnh thoảng có bị khó khăn về ngôn ngữ, cháu vẫn đang rất cố gắng và tiến bộ mỗi ngày. Hãy tiếp tục như thế nhé!

Trân trọng,

Your Child Is Not Performing Up to Ability

Dear Parent or Guardian,

Though your child is smart and capable, he or she is not performing up to his or her ability. We understand that it's difficult to learn when you don't speak the language, but the only way to learn is to try, and your child needs to try harder. If you have any questions, please stop by before or just after school, or give me a call anytime.

Sincerely,

Kính gởi Quý Phụ Huynh hay Người Giám Hộ,

Dù rằng con của quý vị thông minh và có năng lực nhưng cháu không học hết khả năng của mình. Chúng tôi hiểu rằng việc học rất khó khăn khi không nói được tiếng Anh, nhưng cách duy nhất để học là cố gắng và con của quý vị cần phải cố gắng nhiều hơn nữa. Nếu quý vị có thắc mắc, xin ghé vào trước hay sau giờ học, hay gọi cho tôi vào bất cứ lúc nào.

Trân trọng,

Please Schedule a Meeting

Dear Parent or Guardian,

Please call or stop by the school office to schedule a meeting concerning your child. We understand that your time is valuable, but this is very important.

Sincerely,

Kính gởi Quý Phụ Huynh hay Người Giám Hộ,

Xin gọi hay ghé văn phòng nhà trường để ấn định buổi họp về con của quý vị. Chúng tôi hiểu rằng thời giờ của quý vị rất quý báu nhưng đây là việc rất quan trọng.

Trân trọng,

I am the parent of _____.

Tôi là phụ huynh của _____.

❏ *Tôi cần một thông ngôn viên.*

❏ I need a translator.

Your Child's Behavior Is a Problem

Dear Parent or Guardian,

Your child's behavior is unacceptable. Not only does your child create an environment where he or she cannot learn, but your child is also disrupting the learning of others. I hope we can work as a team to help your child learn to behave appropriately in school. If your child continues his or her current behavior, it will result in severe disciplinary action. If you have any questions, please stop by before or just after school, or give me a call anytime.

Sincerely,

Kính gởi Quý Phụ Huynh hay Người Giám Hộ,

Hành vi của con quý vị không thể chấp nhận được. Không những cháu tạo môi trường cho chính cháu không thể học được, mà còn phá việc học của những bạn khác. Tôi hy vọng chúng ta có thể cùng nhau hợp tác nhằm giúp cháu biết cư xử phù hợp trong nhà trường. Nếu vẫn tiếp tục có những hành vi như thế, thì có thể cháu sẽ bị kỷ luật nặng. Nếu quý vị có thắc mắc, xin ghé vào trước hoặc sau giờ học, hay gọi cho tôi vào bất cứ lúc nào.

Trân trọng,

Absences Are Hurting Performance

Dear Parent or Guardian,

Your child's absences are hurting his or her performance. Much of what we do in school builds on what we did the day before; if a student is absent it can be very hard to catch up. I hope that we can work together as a team to help make sure that your child attends class. If you have any questions, please stop by before or just after school, or give me a call anytime.

Sincerely,

Kính gởi Quý Phụ Huynh hay Người Giám Hộ,

Việc nghỉ học của con quý vị sẽ ảnh hưởng đến thành tích học tập của cháu. Phần lớn những gì chúng ta học ở trường là dựa vào những điều mà chúng ta học hôm trước; học sinh nào vắng mặt sẽ rất khó theo kịp bài vở. Tôi hy vọng chúng ta có thể cùng nhau hợp tác để chắc là con của quý vị có đi học. Nếu quý vị có thắc mắc, xin ghé vào trước hoặc sau giờ học hay gọi cho tôi vào bất cứ lúc nào.

Trân trọng,

Tardiness Is Hurting Performance

Dear Parent or Guardian,

Your child is frequently late to class, and this tardiness is hurting his or her performance. By missing the beginning of the period, your child misses important directions and information, making it impossible for him or her to keep up with the rest of the class. I hope that we can work together as a team to help make sure that your child attends class. If you have any questions, please stop by before or just after school, or give me a call anytime.

Sincerely,

Kính gởi Quý Phụ Huynh hay Người Giám Hộ,

Con của quý vị thường xuyên đi học trễ, và việc này ảnh hưởng đến thành tích học tập của cháu. Do bỏ không học từ lúc đầu nên cháu bỏ lỡ các chỉ dẫn và thông tin quan trọng làm cho cháu không thể nào theo kịp các bạn khác. Tôi hy vọng chúng ta có thể cùng nhau hợp tác để chắc là con của quý vị có đi học. Nếu quý vị có thắc mắc, xin ghé vào trước hoặc sau giờ học hay gọi cho tôi vào bất cứ lúc nào.

Trân trọng,

General Resources That School Offers

Dear Parent or Guardian,

The teachers and staff here at school hope to help you and your child in any way we can. The school offers translators and may also be able to help with school supplies and other services. Please feel free to stop by the school office anytime to explore the services available. If you work during the day, you can always call or send a note with your child. We hope to talk to you soon!

Sincerely,

Kính gởi Quý Phụ Huynh hay Người Giám Hộ,

Giáo viên và nhân viên ở trường hy vọng được giúp quý vị và con của quý vị bằng bất cứ cách nào. Nhà trường có thông dịch viên và có thể cung cấp tiếp liệu và các dịch vụ khác. Xin đừng ngần ngại ghé vào văn phòng nhà trường vào bất cứ lúc nào để hỏi thêm về những dịch vụ sẵn có. Nếu làm việc cả ngày, quý vị có thể gọi hay gởi tin cho con mình. Chúng tôi hy vọng sớm được nói chuyện với quý vị!

Trân trọng,

3

Hmong

Hla dej yuav hle khau—Tsiv teb tsaws chaw yuav hle hau

(When you cross a river, take off your sandals—When you leave your country, take off your hat)

CULTURAL FACTS

Hmong in the United States

The homeland of the Hmong ethnic group includes the mountains of southern China and stretches as far south as Laos, Thailand, and northern Vietnam. Concerted Hmong immigration to the United States began in 1976, mostly in response to Laotian persecution and as an effect of the Vietnam War. By the 2000 census, 270,000 Hmong were living in the United States. Just 40 percent of those over twenty-four years of age have completed high school and about 7 percent have completed four or more years of college. This relative lack of schooling among Hmong immigrants results from a primarily agricultural background, a lack of access to schools, and the forced displacement and disruption many Hmong have experienced. Almost 40 percent of all Hmong families live below the poverty level. The highest concentrations of Hmong in the United States live in California, Minnesota, and Wisconsin, specifically in Fresno, Minneapolis, Madison, and Milwaukee.

The Hmong Language

The term "Hmong" applies to a number of dialects, many of which are not mutually intelligible. The most common dialect is the White Hmong, also known as the *Hmong Daw*; others include the Black Hmong and the Blue Hmong. Although the Hmong language may have had a written form long ago, it has been exclusively oral for more than four thousand years

(Mote, 2004). It was not until 1959 that Shong Lue Yang, a Laotian farmer and teacher, introduced a writing system for Hmong, using an alphabet that he claimed was given to him by God.

Hmong Religion and Culture

During the colonial period, Catholic and Protestant missionaries converted many of the Hmong to Christianity. While approximately half the American Hmong population identifies itself as Christian, the other half embraces its original religious practices of animistic shamanism. To this second group, the spiritual world coexists with the physical world, which is filled with ancestral, house, and nature spirits, both good and bad (Grimmett, 2003). Within Asia, Hmongs were frequently forced to uphold the state religion, which was usually Buddhism. Hmong political leaders were mindful to respect Buddhism for political reasons, but local communities often abandoned these practices in more private settings.

Hmong Holidays and Other Important Days

Traditionally, the only Hmong holiday is the New Year celebration, which takes place in December during the two darkest weeks of the year. During this time, all the spirits who helped during the year are thanked and there are feasts, dances, and games. In the United States, Hmong New Year's celebrations occur any time between September and January, frequently coinciding with Thanksgiving or winter breaks. Though holidays are scarce, the Hmong place great importance on ceremonies, which are performed to commemorate births, deaths, and agricultural events.

Pronunciation and Alphabet

Of the languages included in this book, Hmong is one of the most difficult to pronounce, as complex differences in intonation and pitch can change word meaning. Every Hmong word is monosyllabic and ends in a vowel. The consonants you will notice at the end of written Hmong words indicate intonation only, and are never pronounced. Keep in mind that this language challenge works in reverse as well, and your Hmong students will need significant support in learning to pronounce English. In the dictionaries that follow, tones are indicated using the following guide:

1—high tone

2—falling tone

3—midtone, slightly higher than your regular speaking pitch

4—your regular speaking pitch

5—rising tone

6—elongated rising tone

7—falling, breathy tone

8—truncated tone that ends in a glottal stop

Communication With Home: Useful Phrases

English	Hmong	Pronunciation Guide
Parents	Niam txiv	Nia^8 tzee^5
Mother	Niam	Nia^8
Father	Txiv	Tzee^5
Aunt	Phauj (paternal) Niam tais (maternal)	Pao^2 Nia^8 dye^4
Uncle	Txiv ntxawm (younger uncle) Txiv hlob (older uncle) (paternal) Dab laug (maternal)	Tzee^5 ntzer^8 Tzee^5 hlaw^1 Daa^1 lao^7
Brother	Boys: Tij laug (older brother), Kwv (younger brother) Girls: Nus	Dee^2 lao^7 Goo^5 Nuu^4
Sister	Girls: Niam laus (older sister) Niam hluas (younger sister) Boys: Muam	Nia^8 lao^4 Nia^8 hlua^4 Mua^8
Cousin	Kwv tij	Goo^5 dee^8
Boyfriend/Girlfriend	Hluas nraug/Hluas nkauj	Hlua^4 ndrao^7/Hlua^4 ngao^2
Whom do you live with?	Koj nrog leej twg nyob?	Gaw^2 ndraw^7 leng^2 doo^7 nyaw^1?
What is your phone number?	Koj tus naj npawb xov tooj yog li cas?	Gaw^2 doo^4 number saw^5 tong^2 yao^7 daa^1 gee^3?
Please show this note to your ____.	Thov muab daim ntawv no rau koj ____ xyuas.	Taw^5 mua^1 dye^8 ndau^5 naw^3 drau^3 ____ shua^4.
Please get this signed and bring it back.	Thov xee npe rau tag nqa rov qab los.	Taw^5 seng^4 nbay^4 drau^4 daa^7 ngaa^4 draw^5 gaa^1 law^4.
Please have your ____ call me at school.	Thov kom koj ____ hu xov tooj rau kuv tom tsev kawm ntawv.	Taw^5 gaw^8 gaw^2 ____ who^3 saw^5 dong^2 drau^4 goo^5 daw^8 jay^5 guh^8-ndau^5.

Classroom Communication: Useful Phrases

English	Hmong	Pronunciation Guide
Sit down please.	Thov zaum.	Taw[5] zhow[8].
The assignment is on the board.	Txoj hauj lwm nyob tim daim kab das.	Dsaw[2] how[2] lue[8] nyaw[1] dee[8] dye[8] gaa[1] daa[4].
Pay attention!	Ua twb zoo mloog!	Ooha[3] due[1] zhong[3] mlong[7]!
Good job.	Zoo.	Zhong[3].
Excellent!	Zoo kawg nkaus!	Zhong[3] guh[7] ngau[4]!
Do you need help?	Koj puas xav tau kev pab?	Gaw[2] bua[4] saa[5] tao[8] keng[7] baa[1]?
Do you understand?	Koj puas to taub?	Gaw[2] bua[4] daw[3] dau[1]?
Do you understand the assignment?	Koj puas to taub txoj hauj lwm?	Gaw[2] bua[4] daw[3] dau[1] tzaw[2] hau[2] lue[8]?
Thanks for listening.	Ua tsaug rau koj mloog.	Ooha[3] jao[7] drao[3] kaw[5] mlong[7].
Open your book to page ____.	Thuav koj phau ntawv rau phab ____.	Tua[5] gaw[2] pao[3] ndaw[5] drao[3] paa[1] ____.
I know it's hard; do the best you can.	Kuv paub tias nyuab; ua raws li koj ua tau.	Gue[5] bau[1] dee-uh[4] nyua[1]; ooha[3] druh[4] lee[3] gaw[2] ooha[3] dao[3].
How do you say ____ in Hmong?	Lus Hmoob hais ____ li cas?	Lew[4] Hmong[1] hi[4] ____ lee[3] chuh[4]?
What do you think about ____?	Koj xav li cas hais txog ____?	Gaw[2] saa[5] lee[3] chuh[4] hi[4] tzaw[7] ____?
I would like you to ____.	Kuv xav kom koj ____.	Gue[5] saa[4] gaw[8] gaw[2] ____.
Do you know how to ____?	Koj puas paub ua ____ ua li cas?	Gaw[2] bua[4] bao[1] ooha[3] ____ ooha[3] lee[3] chuh[4]?
Is this easy or hard?	Ua qhov no yooj yim los nyuab?	Ooha[3] kaw[5] naw[3] yong[2] yee[8] law[4] nyua[1]?
Quiet, please.	Thov, tswm seeb.	Taw[5], jue[8] sheng[1].
Please be careful.	Thov xyuam xim.	Taw[5] shoua[8] see[8].

Student Communication: Useful Phrases

English	Hmong	Pronunciation Guide
I am new.	Kuv tuaj tshiab.	Goo[5] dewuh[2] chia[1].
I don't speak English.	Kuv tsis paub hais lus Askiv.	Goo[5] jee[4] bao[1] hi[4] lou[4] aagee[5].
Do you speak ____?	Koj puas paub hais lus ____?	Gaw[2] bua[4] bao[1] hi[4] lou[4] ____?
I'm from ____.	Kuv tuaj ____ tuaj.	Goo[5] doouh[2] ____ doouh[2].
I'm sorry.	Kuv thov zam txim.	Goo[5] taw[5] zhaa[8] tzee[8].
Excuse me.	Thov txim.	Taw[5] tzee[8].
Thanks.	Ua tsaug.	Oouh[3] jao[7].
My name is ____.	Kuv lub npe hu ua ____.	Goo[5] lou[1] nbay[3] who[3] oouh[3] ____.
Can you help me?	Koj pab kuv puas tau?	Gaw[2] baa[1] goo[5] bua[4] dow[3]?
Where is the ____?	____ nyob qhov twg?	____ nyaw[1] ghaw[5] tou[7]?
Can I play?	Kuv nrog nej ua si puas tau?	Goo[5] ndraw[7] nay[2] ooha[3] she[3] bua[4] dao[3]

Classroom Supplies: Class Dictionary

Book	Computer	Crayons	Eraser
Phau ntawv pao³ ndaw⁵	Khoos phuj tawj kong⁴ pew² duh²	Cov cwj mem zas jaw⁵ jou² meg⁸ za⁴	Lub yas lwv lou¹ yaa⁴ lew⁵
Folder	Glue	Markers	Note
Plhaub khaws ntawv plough¹ kuh⁴ ndaw⁵	Kua nplaum kor³ blau⁸	Cwj mem kos duab cjue² may⁸ gaw⁴ dewuh¹	Daim ntawv sau dye⁸ ndaw⁵ shao³
Notebook	Paint	Paperclip	Pen
Phau ntawv sau pao³ ndaw⁵ shao³	Tsos jaw⁴	Koob tais ntawv gong¹ dye⁴ ndaw⁵	Cwj mem cjue² may⁸
Pencil	Piece of Paper	Poster	Printer
Xaum sao⁸	Daim ntawv dye⁸ ndaw⁵	Daim duab loj loj dye⁸ doouh¹ law² law²	(Lub) luam ntawv (lou) lua ndaw
Ruler	Scissors	Stapler	Tape
(Tus) pas ntsuas (dou⁴) baa⁴ njua⁴	Rab txiab draa¹ tzia¹	Tus tom ntawv dou⁴ daw⁸ ndaw⁵	Ntaub nplaum n·tau¹ blau⁸

School Mechanics: Class Dictionary

Absent	Bathroom	Bell	Cafeteria
Khaj (ntawv) kaa^2 (ndaw^5)	Tsev dej jay^5 day^2	(Lub) tswb (lu) jue^1	Chav tsev noj mov chaa^5 jay^5 naw^2 maw^5
Class Period	**Clock**	**Counselor**	**To Get a Drink**
(Ib) xuab moo kawm ntawv (e) sua^1 mong^3 guh^8 ndaw^5	Lub moo lou^1 mong^3	(Tus) kws pab tswv yim (tu) goo^4 baa^1 jue^5 yee^8	Haus dej how^4 day^2
Gymnasium	**Library**	**Locker**	**Lunch**
Chau ua si Chaa^5 ooha^5 she^3	(Lub) tsev rau ntawv (lu) jay^5 drao^3 ndaw^5	(Lub) chaw (rau khoom) (lou) chaw (drao goo^8)	Pluas su blua^4 shoe^3
Office	**Playground**	**Principal**	**Recess**
Lub look am lou^1 long^3 gaa^8	Chaw ua si sure^3 or^3 shee^3	(Tus) thaj khu (tu) taa^2 kou^3	Caij so ua si cjai^2 shaw^3 ooa^3 she^3
Schedule	**Secretary**	**Tardy**	**Teacher**
8:30 Welcome/Class Business 9:00 Language Arts 10:30 Mathematics 11:30 Social Studies 12:00 Lunch 1:00 Science 2:00 Art/Music/PE			
Daim ntawv swb sij hawm dai ndaw shoe shi huh	(Tus) teev ntawv (tus) te^4 ndaw^5	Tuaj lig dewuh^2 lee^7	Nais Khu nigh^4 kou^3

Assignment Words: Class Dictionary

Assignment	Correct	Design (Plan)	Directions
Hauj lwm hao[2] lue[8]	Raug drao[7]	Tawm tswv yim duh[8] jue[5] yee[8]	Cov kev taw qhia cjaw[5] gay[5] duh[3] queea[3]
To Discuss	To Draw	Due Date	Grade
Sib tham shaa[1] taa[2]	Kos duab gaw[4] doouh[1]	Hnub kawg hnou[1] guh[7]	(Tus) khab nia (dew[4]) kaa[1] nia[3]
To Help	Homework	To Listen	Permission Letter
Pab baa[1]	Cov ntawv ua tom tsev cjaw[5] ndaw[5] ooha[3] daw[8] jay[5]	Mloog mlong[7]	Daim ntawv tso cai dye[8] ndaw[5] jaw[3] cjai[3]
Questions	To Read	Stop	To Take Notes
Lus nug lou[4] new[7]	Nyeem nyeng[8]	Nres ndray[4]	Sau ntawv shao[3] ndaw[5]
Test	To Turn In	To Write	Wrong
(Kev) xeem ntawv (gay[5]) sang[8] ndaw[5]	Xa rov qab saa[3] draw[5] ghaa[1]	Sau shao[3]	Tsis raug gee[4] drao[7]

Playground and Physical Education Vocabulary: Class Dictionary

Ball	Baseball	Basketball	To Catch
(Lub) npas	Cuam npa (baseball)	Pov npa (basketball)	Txais
(lou[1]) nbaa[4]	jua[8] pao[3] (baseball)	baw[5] baw[3] (basketball)	tzai[4]

To Change	Circle	Drill	Field
Hloov	(Lub) voj voog	Xyaum	Tiaj (tshav)
hlong[5]	(lou[1]) vaw[2] vong[7]	syouh[8]	dia[2] (chaa[5])

To Follow	Football (American)	Four Square	Go in Front
Lawv qab	Ncaws npa (football)	Plaub lub duab plaub fab	Mus tom hauv ntej
luh[5] gaa[1]	n-cjuh[4] nbaw[3] (football)	plau[1] luu[1] dor[1] plau[1] fa[1]	mu[4] taw[8] hau[5] n·taa[2]

Gym Clothes	Handball	To Hit	Hurt
Khaub ncaws (ntaus, ncaw) npa	Pob tes ńtaus	Ntaus	Raug mob
cow[1] ncjow[4] (dao, jaw) baa[4]	paw[1] taa[4] n·tau[4]	ndao[4]	drao[7] maw[1]

To Jump	Jumprope	Kickball	Line
Dhia	Hlua dhia	Pob taw ncaws	(Ua) kab
teeuh[3]	h·lor[3] dhee-e[3]	paw[1] ter[3] n-cjuh[4]	(ua) gaa[1]

(Continued)

(Continued)

Lock	Locker Room	To Lose	Out of Bounds
(Lub) ntsuas phoov (lou[1]) njua[4] pong[5]	(Lub) chav rau khoom (lou[1]) chaa[5] drao[3] kong[8]	Swb shoe[1]	Tawm sab nraud tus ciam duh[8] shaa[1] ndrao[6] do[4] cjia[8]
The Rules Cov cai cjaw[5] cjai[3]	To Run Khiav keeuh[5]	Shoes Khau cow[3]	Sideline (Tus) ciam teb (dew[4]) cjia[8] day[1]
Soccer Ncaws npa ncjuh[4] nbaa[4]	Sport Ua kis las ooha[3] gey[4] laa[4]	To Stretch Ncab ib ce njyaa[1] e[1] cjay[3]	Team Pawg neeg baa[1] neng[7]
Tetherball Pob khi hlua paw[1] khee[3] h·lor[3]	To Throw Pov baw[5]	Volleyball Ntaus npa ndao[4] nbaa[4]	Whistle (Lub) xuav (lou[1]) sao[5]

The Rules content: RULES — The ckoskd cidij ekd ckdou. Kndk dui idu nduy. Liehy djsuikll giehd ckdiiy clidusk Idicjy djywo dlcisdj bldinueodk cldiin uey Ecly dlihdyope. giehd ckdiiy clidusk

Science Vocabulary: Class Dictionary

Acid	Animal	Base	Climate
Kua qaub (acid) goouh[3] ghow[1]	Tsiaj jeeuh[2]	Kua tsis qaub goouh[3] jee[4] ghow[1]	Huab cua hua[1] cjueuh[3]
Dinosaur	**Earth**	**Electricity**	**Energy**
(Tus) tsiaj Dinosaur (tus) jia dinosaur	Ntiaj teb n·tee-e[2] taa[1]	Hluavtaws xob h·lor[5] ter[4] saw[1]	Lub zog lou[1] zaw[7]
Environment	**Experiment**	**Extinct**	**Hypothesis**
Thai chaw ib puaq nciq taa[2] chuh[3] e[1] booha[7] n-gee[7]	Kev sim gay[5] she[8]	Tu noob do[3] nong[1]	Kev xav gay[5] saa[5]
To Investigate	**Lab Notebook**	**Laboratory**	**Matter**
Tshawb nrhiav cher[1] n·tee-e[5]	Phau ntawv sau pao[3] ndaw[5] shao[3]	Chav sim chaa[5] she[8]	Khoom tseeb khong[8] t-seng[1]
Motion	**Planet**	**Plant**	**Science**
Ua zog or[3] zaw[7]	Lub ntuj lou[1] ndew[2]	Ib tsob ntoo mos e[1] jaw[1] ndong[3] maw[3]	Txuj ci tzew[2] chee[3]

Math Vocabulary: Class Dictionary

To Add	Answer	To Calculate	Calculator
Sib ntxiv ji tse	$1 + 1 = ②$ (Los) lus teb (lo) lu day[1]	$\begin{array}{r}7\\8\\+5\\\hline 20\end{array}$ Xam lej saa[8] lay[2]	Lub tshuab xam lej lou[1] choua[1] saa[8] lay[2]
To Combine	**To Divide**	**Equation**	**Exponent**
Sib tov ua ke shi[3] to oouh[3] gay[3]	$\div$ Sib faib shi fye[1]	$2 + 3 = 5$ Sib npaug, ob sab sib npaug shi bqo, oo saa[8] shi pua[2]	A^4 Lej npaug (exponent) lay[2] n-bao[7]
Graph	**Math**	**To Multiply**	**Numbers**
Daim duab qhia dye[8] doouh[1] ghia[3]	Kev xam lej gay[5] saa[8] lay[2]	$3 ⊗ 2$ Zauv, lej sib tshooj zao le shi chong[2]	$1\ 2\ 3\ 4\ 5$ $6\ 7\ 8\ 9$ Leb lay[1]
To Order	**Problem**	**Property**	**To Prove**
$1, 2, 3, 4$ Tu dew[3]	$1 + 3 = ?$ Teeb meem zauv,leb te meng zao le	$x(y + 2)$ Yam khoom zauv, leb goo sao zao le (property)	Sim Ua she[8] oouh[3]
To Simplify	**To Solve**	**To Subtract**	**Variable**
$\frac{3X + 42}{4} = 6X \rightarrow X = 2$ Ua kom me oouh[3] gaw[8] may[3]	$3x=12$ $X=4$ Daws teeb meem duh[4] deng[1] meng[8]	$12 ⊖ 6$ Rho tawm trhaw[3] duwh[8]	x, y Zauv,leb hloov zao le variable

Social Studies Vocabulary: Class Dictionary

Africa	Asia	Australia	Buddhist
Teb chaws Africa day[1] chuh[4] Africa	Esxias a sia (Asia)	Ovstaslias os[5] st-a[4] -lee-e[4]	Neeg ntseeg hauj sam neng[7] njang[7] how[2] shaa[8]
Christian	Citizenship	Continent	Country
Neeg ntseeg yexus neng[7] njang[7] yay[3] sue[4]	Kev ua pejxeem ke[5] or[3] pe[2]-seng[8]	(Daim) thooj av loj (dye[8]) tong[2] aa[5] law[2]	(Lub) teb chaws (lou[1]) day[1] chuh[4]
Democracy	Europe	Geography	Government
Kev cai ywj pheej ke[5] jii[3] you[2] peng[2]	Teb chaw (Europe) te jaw (Europe)	Liaj ia teb chaw, toj roob hauv pes txog lub ntiaj teb lea ia te jaw, to roo hao pe tso lu ndia te	Tseem fwv tseng[8] fou[5]
Hinduism	History	Jewish	Map
Kev dabqhuas heesdus ke[5] da[1] q-hor[4] heng[4]-duu[4]	Liv xwm li swh	Neeg yudais neng[7] you[3] dye[4]	Ntawv qhia kev ndaw qia ge
Muslim	North American	South America	World
Neeg Muslim neng[7] muslim	Amelikas qaum teb America gao[8] day[1]	Amelikas qab teb America gaa[1] day[1]	(Lub) ntiaj teb (lou[1]) (ndia te) ndeeuh[2] day[1]

Welcome to My Classroom

Dear Parent or Guardian,

I would like to welcome your child to my classroom. The first couple of weeks can be difficult for students who don't yet speak English, but by working with you as a team I hope to make the transition as smooth as possible. While my Hmong is not strong, I will do the best I can to communicate what is expected of your child in the classroom and in the school. Please feel free to stop by before or just after school, or to call anytime.

Again, welcome to our school! I look forward to speaking with you soon.

Sincerely,

Nyob zoo Niam Txiv los yog tus Tsom Kwm,

Kuv zoo siab txais tos koj tus menyuam tuaj kawm ntawv rau hauv kuv chav qhia ntawv. Thawj ob peb lub lwm tiam tom ntej no tej zaum yuav nyuab heev rau cov menyuam uas tsis paub lus Askiv, tab sis kuv cia siab tia yog koj thiab kuv wb koom tes ua kev lawm, nws yuav ua tau ib txog kev yooj yim rau koj tus me nyuam txoj kev kawm. Txawm tias kuv cov lus Hmoob tsis zoo los kuv yuav hais li kuv hais tau kom pab tau koj tus menyuam nkag siab txog txoj kev kawm ntawv thiab nws yuav ua li cas thiaj kawm ntawv tau nyob rau hauv tsev kawm ntawv. Yog koj xav paub dab tsi, thov txhob ua siab deb, tuaj hauv tsev kawm ntawv ua ntej kawm ntawv los sis tom qab thaum lawb ntawv lawm, los yog hu xov tooj rau kuv thaum twg los tau.

Thov tos txais koj tus menyuam ib zaug ntxiv dua! Xav tias yuav tau nrog koj sib tham sai sai no.

Sau Npe,

Your Child Is a Pleasure to Have in Class

Dear Parent or Guardian,

This is a note of thanks to let you know that your child is a pleasure to have in class, and to thank you for the work you do at home to help your child succeed. Though your child sometimes has difficulties with the language, he or she is trying hard and making progress every day. Keep up the good work!

Sincerely,

Nyob zoo Niam Txiv los yog tus Tsom kwm,

Ntawm no yog ib daim ntawv ua tsaug qhia koj paub tias kuv zoo siab uas koj tus menyuam tau los kawm ntawv rau hauv kuv chav tsev qhia ntawv. Txawm hais tias muaj zaum puav koj tus menyuam tsis paub lus zoo, los nws yeej mob siab thiab sib zog kawm txhua txhua hnub. Txhawb nws kom kawm zoo zoo!

Sau npe,

Your Child Is Not Performing Up to Ability

Dear Parent or Guardian,

Though your child is smart and capable, he or she is not performing up to his or her ability. We understand that it's difficult to learn when you don't speak the language, but the only way to learn is to try, and your child needs to try harder. If you have any questions, please stop by before or just after school, or give me a call anytime.

Sincerely,

Nyob zoo Niam Txiv los yog tus Tsom Kwm,

Txawm tias koj tus menyuam ntse thiab muaj peev xwm heeb los nws tseem tsis tau kawm nca cuag raws li nws lub peev xwm. Peb yeej to taub zoo tias yog ib tug neeg twg tsis paub luag cov lus ces nws yeej kawm nyuab, tab sis qhov ua yuav pab tau koj tus menyuam yog yuav tswm kom nws sib sib zog kawm. Yog koj muaj lus nug, tuaj hauv tsev kawm ntawv ua ntej kawm ntawv los sis tom qab lawb ntawv lawm, los yog hu xov tooj tuaj rau kuv tau txhua txhua lub sij hawm.

Sau npe,

Please Schedule a Meeting

Dear Parent or Guardian,

Please call or stop by the school office to schedule a meeting concerning your child. We understand that your time is valuable, but this is very important.

Sincerely,

Nyob zoo Niam Txiv los yog tus Tsom kwm,

Thov hu xov tooj los sis tuaj teem caij hauv tsev kawm ntawv es yuav sib tham txog koj tus menyuam. Peb yeej paub tias koj lub sij hawm muaj nqi heev, tab sis qhov no yog ib yam hauj lwm tseem ceeb heev.

Sau npe,

I am the parent of _____

Kuv yog _____ niam (losyog txiv)

❑ I need a translator.

❑ Kuv xav tau ib tug neeg txhais lus.

Your Child's Behavior Is a Problem

Dear Parent or Guardian,

Your child's behavior is unacceptable. Not only does your child create an environment where he or she cannot learn, but your child is also disrupting the learning of others. I hope we can work as a team to help your child learn to behave appropriately in school. If your child continues his or her current behavior, it will result in severe disciplinary action. If you have any questions, please stop by before or just after school, or give me a call anytime.

Sincerely,

Nyob zoo Niam Txiv los yog tus Tsom kwm,

Koj tus menyuam coj tau ib tug cwj pwm yuav tsis tau kiag li. Tsis yog hais tias qhov no yuav rau nws kawm ntawv tsis tau ntawv xwb, tab sis nws tseem ua kom meem txom luag leej lwm tus txoj kev kawm thiab. Kuv vam khom tias peb yuav sib koom tes ua ke pab qhuab qhia kom koj tus menyuam coj tau ib tug cwj pwm zoo nyob rau hauv tsev kawm ntawv. Yog koj tus menyuam pheej coj tus cwj pwm zoo li no mus xwb, ntshai yuav tau xyuas ib txoj kev raug txim tseem ceeb rau nws. Yog koj muaj lus nug, tuaj hauv tsev kawm ntawv ua ntej kawm ntawv los sis yav tom qab thaum lawb ntawv lawm, los yog hu xov tooj tuaj rau kuv thaum twg los tau.

Sau Npe,

Absences Are Hurting Performance

Dear Parent or Guardian,

Your child's absences are hurting his or her performance. Much of what we do in school builds on what we did the day before; if a student is absent it can be very hard to catch up. I hope that we can work together as a team to help make sure that your child attends class. If you have any questions, please stop by before or just after school, or give me a call anytime.

Sincerely,

Nyob zoo Niam Txiv los yog tus Tsom Kwm,

Koj tus menyuam txoj kev khaj ntawv ua rau nws txoj kev kawm poob qab zuj zuj. Ntau ntau yam uas peb ua hauv tsev kawm ntawv yog los ntawm tej yam uas peb xub kawm ua ntej ob peb hnub los lawm; yog ib tug menyuam khaj ntawv lawm yuav kawm kom raws tau luag lwm tus mas nyuab kawg nkaus. Kuv vam khom tias peb yuav sib koom tes kom pab tau koj tus menyuam tuaj kawm ntawv kom cuag ncua. Yog koj muaj lus nug, tuaj hauv tsev kawm ntawv ua ntej kawm ntawv los sis tom qab thaum lawb ntawv lawm, los yog hu xov tooj rau kuv thaum twg los tau.

Sau Npe,

Tardiness Is Hurting Performance

Dear Parent or Guardian,

Your child is frequently late to class, and this tardiness is hurting his or her performance. By missing the beginning of the period, your child misses important directions and information, making it impossible for him or her to keep up with the rest of the class. I hope that we can work together as a team to help make sure that your child attends class. If you have any questions, please stop by before or just after school, or give me a call anytime.

Sincerely,

Nyob zoo Niam Txiv los yog tus Tsom Kwm,

Koj tus menyuam pheej tuaj kawm ntawv lig feem ntau tag li xwb, qhov no ua rau koj tus menyuam txoj kev kawm poob qab. Yog koj tus menyuam khaj ntawv lub sib hawm thib ib lawm ces ua rau koj tus menyuam plam cov lus qhia ua ntaub ntawv thiab nws yuav tsis paub cov xov tseem ceeb ua yuav los pab rau nws ua tau nws cov ntaub ntawv ncav cuag nws cov phooj ywg. Kuv vam khom tias peb yuav sib koom tes ua hauj lwm ua ke kom paub tau meej meej tias koj tus menyuam tuaj kawm ntawv. Yog koj muaj lus nug, tuaj hauv tsev kawm ntawv ua ntej kawm ntawv los sis tom qab thaum lawb ntawv lawm, los yog hu xov tooj rau kuv thaum twg los tau.

Sau Npe,

General Resources That School Offers

Dear Parent or Guardian,

The teachers and staff here at school hope to help you and your child in any way we can. The school offers translators and may also be able to help with school supplies and other services. Please feel free to stop by the school office anytime to explore the services available. If you work during the day, you can always call or send a note with your child. We hope to talk to you soon!

Sincerely,

Nyob zoo Niam Txiv los yog tus Tsom kwm,

Cov xib fwb qhia ntawv thiab peb cov neeg ua hauj lwm nyob rau hauv tsev kawm ntawv no txaus siab yuav pab koj thiab koj tus menyuam li peb pab tau. Peb lub tsev kawm ntawv muaj neeg txhais lus thiab tej zaum peb muaj khoom plig cuab yeej kawm ntawv thiab lwm yam kev pab pub rau nej. Thov caw nej tuaj xyuas peb loo kam thaum twg los tau, kom nej thiaj pom tias peb muaj kev pab dab tsi rau nej. Yog koj ua hauj lwm nruab hnub lawm, koj hu xov tooj los sis sau ib daim ntawv rau koj tus menyuam nqa tuaj xwb los tau. Peb vam tias yuav tau nrog koj tham sai sai no!

Sau Npe,

4

Chinese (Cantonese)

Shan bu zhuan lu zhuan

(If the mountain doesn't move, move the route around the mountain)

CULTURAL FACTS

Chinese in the United States

The Chinese were one of the first minority ethnic groups to come to the United States, and for this reason there exists a strong Chinese American support network for more recent immigrants and a robust population of native Cantonese speakers. However, the Chinese American population remains largely divided based on date of immigration. For example, cities with large Chinese American populations such as New York, San Francisco, Los Angeles, Houston, and Philadelphia frequently have two Chinatowns: the traditional one and a newer one that is populated with immigrants from the 1960s and 1970s. In addition to the big cities, smaller pockets of Chinese Americans are also dispersed in rural towns, often near a university, throughout the United States. According to the 2000 census, people of Chinese descent were more likely than the average population to have earned a bachelor's degree (over two-thirds of those born in the United States and half of those born abroad have) and to have graduated from high school (88 percent of all Chinese in America have). The Chinese American population continues to grow rapidly due to immigration, but the average birth rate is lower than that of American whites. Recently, adoption of babies from mainland China has also helped to increase the Chinese American population, though most of these adoptions are by white parents.

The Chinese Language

There are two Chinese languages—Mandarin and Cantonese. While Mandarin is the official language of mainland China and is the twelfth most common language spoken by ELL students in the United States, this chapter focuses on Cantonese, which is the primary language of Southern China. Some consider Cantonese a dialect, containing within it many more dialects. The most common Cantonese dialect is *Guangzhou*, which is spoken by about 70 million people worldwide and is the primary dialect of recent U.S. immigrants from Southern China. Guangzhou continues to be widely spoken even by third-generation Chinese Americans of Cantonese ancestry. Spoken Chinese is a tonal language, meaning that differences in pitch indicate different words.

Chinese Religion and Culture

As would be expected in a country of over 1.3 billion people, religion and culture vary widely across China. And today's China is changing at a pace never before seen. As industry supplants agrarianism, so too are Western influences vying with traditional ways of thought, at times creating cultural and political friction. Traditionally, Mahayana Buddhism has been China's most prevalent religion, frequently tinged with Taoism and Chinese folk religion. Many Westerners find this religious plurality confusing even without the secular contribution of Confucianism, which has helped shape the national character since the fifth century BCE. Commonalities among these ways of thought include ancestor worship, respect for authority, and the importance of family. Chinese culture, too, has a complex history, including rich traditions of art, music, science, and scholarship in every field of study. In both religious and secular life, China has traditionally respected the idea of balance—yin and yang—and the importance of integration within the group.

Chinese Holidays and Other Important Days

Many Chinese holidays are based on the lunar calendar, and thus the dates change from year to year. For this year's dates, search for the festival name on the Internet.

春节: Fireworks, feasts (including ten courses and a whole-fish entrée), and the hanging of a new door god mark *The Chinese New Year*, which is held the first day of the first lunar month.

元宵节: *The Lantern Festival* occurs on the fifteenth day of the first lunar month.

端午节: *The Dragon Boat Festival* is on the fifth day of the fifth lunar month.

七夕: *The Night of Sevens* (the seventh night of the seventh lunar month) is the one night of the year the goddess Zhi Nü can visit her love, the farmer boy Niu Lang.

中秋节: *The Mid-Autumn Festival* or *Moon Festival* occurs on the fifteenth day of the eighth lunar month.

Pronunciation and Alphabet

There are also two versions of the Chinese script—simplified and traditional. This chapter uses the simplified script of mainland China, rather than the traditional form, which is still used by Chinese populations in Taiwan, Hong Kong, and Macao.

The first verifiable record of the Chinese system of writing is found on the oracle bones of the Shang Dynasty, and dated near 1700 BCE. Chinese characters are not pictographs and are not phonetic; rather, they are stylized representations of words, syllables, or other pieces of language. One needs to know about 3,000 characters to read a Chinese newspaper, and an educated person will know more than 5,000 characters. For a more detailed description of Chinese pronunciation, look at one of the following guides:

- *Teach Yourself Cantonese.* Hugh Baker and P. K. Ho. New York: McGraw Hill, 2003.
- *A Practical Chinese-English Pronouncing Dictionary.* Janey Chen and Ena Simms. North Clarendon, VT: Charles E. Tuttle Co., 2003.
- *Chinese (Cantonese).* Philadelphia: Pimsleur Language Programs, 1999.

Communication With Home: Useful Phrases

English	Chinese Script	Pronunciation Guide
Parents	父母	Fu mou
Mother	母親	Mou chan
Father	父親	Fu chan
Aunta	阿姨/姑姑	A yi/Gu gu
Uncle	叔叔/舅舅	Suk suk/Kau kau
Brother	哥哥/弟弟	Go go/Dai dai
Sister	姐姐/妹妹	Ze ze/Mui mui
Cousin	表弟/表妹	Biu dai/Biu mui
Boyfriend/Girlfriend	男朋友/女朋友	Naam pang yau/Neoi pang yau
Whom do you live with?	你跟誰住在一起？	Nei tung bin go zyu yat cai?
What is your phone number?	你的電話號碼幾號？	Nei gei din waa hai mat hou ma?
Please show this note to your ____.	請把這個便條拿給你的 ____ 看。	Ceng ne zoeng bin tiu bei nei gei ____ tai.
Please get this signed and bring it back.	請在這個上頭簽名，然後把它帶回來。	Ceng hai ne dou cim meng, yin hau daai faan lai.
Please have your ____ call me at school.	請你的 ____ 打電話到學校找我。	Ceng nei gei ____ daa din waa dou hok hau wan ngo.

Classroom Communication: Useful Phrases

English	Chinese Script	Pronunciation Guide
Sit down please.	請坐。	Ceng zo.
The assignment is on the board.	作業寫在黑板上。	Zok yip se hai hak baan dou.
Pay attention!	注意！	Zyu yi!
Good job.	做得好。	Zou dak hou.
Excellent!	很棒！	Hou hou!
Do you need help?	你需要幫忙嗎？	Nei seoi yiu bong mong maa?
Do you understand?	你瞭解嗎？	Nei ming baak maa?
Do you understand the assignment?	你瞭解作業嗎？	Nei ming baak zok yip maa?
Thanks for listening.	謝謝你的傾聽。	Do ze nei lau sam teng.
Open your book to page ____.	請把你的書翻到第 ____ 頁。	Zoeng nei bun syu faan dou dai ____ yip.
I know it's hard; do the best you can.	我知道很難；請盡你最大的努力。	Ngo zi dou hou naan; zeon nei zeoi dai nang li zou.
How do you say ____ in Chinese?	____ 用中文怎麼說？	____ zung man dim gong?
What do you think about ____?	你認爲 ____ 如何？	Nei deoi ____ dim seong?
I would like you to ____.	我想要你 ____.	Ngo seong yiu nei ____ .
Do you know how to ____?	你知道如何 ____ 嗎？	Nei zi dou dim ____ maa?
Is this easy or hard?	這個容易還是很難？	Nei go yung yi deng naan?
Quiet, please.	請安靜。	Ceng on zing.
Please be careful.	請仔細點。	Ceng siu sam.

Student Communication: Useful Phrases

English	Chinese Script	Pronunciation Guide
I am new.	我是新來的。	Ngo hai san lai gei.
I don't speak English.	我不會說英語。	Ngo ng wui gong ying man.
Do you speak ____?	你會說 ____ 嗎？	Nei wui gong ____ maa?
I'm from ____.	我是從 ____ 來的。	Ngo hai cung ____ lai.
I'm sorry.	很抱歉。	Ho pou hip.
Excuse me.	對不起。	Deoi ng zyu.
Thanks.	謝謝。	Do ze.
My name is ____.	我的名字叫 ____。	Ngo gei meng giu ____.
Can you help me?	你能幫我嗎？	Nei ho yi bong ngo maa?
Where is the ____?	____ 在哪裡？	____ hai bin dou?
Can I play?	我可以玩嗎？	Ngo ho yi waan maa?

Classroom Supplies: Class Dictionary

Book 教科書 gao fo syu	Computer 電腦 din nou	Crayons 蠟筆 lap b	Eraser 橡皮擦 gaau caat
Folder 文書夾 man gin gaap	Glue 膠水 jiao shwate	Markers 麥克筆 biu gei bat	Note 便條 bin tiu
Notebook 筆記本 bat gei bun	Paint 顏料 ngaan liu	Paperclip 紙夾 zi gaap	Pen 筆 bat
Pencil 鉛筆 yyun bat	Piece of Paper 紙 zi	Poster 海報 hoi bou	Printer 印表機 daa yan gei
Ruler 尺 cek	Scissors 剪刀 gaau zin	Stapler 釘書機 deng syu gei	Tape 帶子 dye zi

School Mechanics: Class Dictionary

Absent	Bathroom	Bell	Cafeteria
曠課	廁所	上課鈴	自助餐廳
kyut zik	ci so	ling	zi zo caan teng

Class Period	Clock	Counselor	To Get a Drink
一堂課	鍾	學生顧問	去喝水
yat tong fo	zung	hok saang gu man	heoi yam seoi

Gymnasium	Library	Locker	Lunch
體育館	圖書館	衣物櫃	午餐
tai yuk gun	tou syu gun	cyu gwai	ng caan

Office	Playground	Principal	Recess
辦公室	運動場	校長	下課
baan gung sat	yuen don chang	haau zoeng	haa fo

Schedule	Secretary	Tardy	Teacher
8:30 Welcome/Class Business 9:00 Language Arts 10:30 Mathematics 11:30 Social Studies 12:00 Lunch 1:00 Science 2:00 Art/Music/PE			
時間表	秘書	遲到	老師
si gaan biu	bei syu	ci dou	lou si

Assignment Words: Class Dictionary

Assignment	Correct	Design	Directions
課外作業 zi ding zok yip	正確 zeng kok	正確 gai waak	指示 syut ming
To Discuss	**To Draw**	**Due Date**	**Grade**
討論 tou leon	畫 waak	截止日期 zit zi yat gei	成績 seng zik
To Help	**Homework**	**To Listen**	**Permission Letter**
協助 bong zo	家庭作業 gaa ting zok yip	聽 teng	同意函 heoi ho seon
Questions	**To Read**	**Stop**	**To Take Notes**
? 問題 man tai	讀 dok	STOP 停止 ting zi	記筆記 gei bat gei
Test	**To Turn In**	**To Write**	**Wrong**
測驗 cak yim	交上 gaau	寫 se	錯誤 cou ng

Playground and Physical Education Vocabulary: Class Dictionary

Ball 球 kau	Baseball 棒球 paang kau	Basketball 籃球 laam kau	To Catch 趕上 gon soeng
To Change 更衣 wun saam	Circle 圓圈 yyun hyun	Drill 練習 lin zaap	Field 運動場 wan dung coeng
To Follow 跟隨 gan ceoi	Football (American) 橄欖球 mei sik zook kau	Four Square 無網四方場地手球遊戲 woe wong si fong charn d show chio yol si	Go in Front 在前面走 zai qian mien zow
Gym Clothes 體育服 tai yuk fuk	Handball 手球遊戲 show chio	To Hit 打擊 daa gik	Hurt 受傷 sau soeng
To Jump 跳 tiu	Jumprope 跳繩 tiao shurn	Kickball 兒童足球 er tang zu chio	Line 隊伍 deoi ng

Lock	Locker Room	To Lose	Out of Bounds
鎖	更衣室	輸	界外
so	gaang yik sat	syu	gaai ngoi
The Rules	To Run	Shoes	Sideline
RULES			
規則	跑	鞋子	界線
kwai zak	paau	haai	gaai sin
Soccer	Sport	To Stretch	Team
足球	運動	伸展	隊
zook kau	wan dung	san zin	deoi
Tetherball	To Throw	Volleyball	Whistle
繩球	丟	排球	口哨
shurn qio	diu	paai kau	hau saau

Science Vocabulary: Class Dictionary

Acid 酸 syun	Animal 動物 dung mat	Base 鹼 gaan	Climate 氣候 hei hau
Dinosaur 恐龍 hung lung	Earth 地球 d chio	Electricity 電 dien	Energy 能源 nang yyun
Environment 環境 waan ging	Experiment 實驗 sat yim	Extinct 絕種 zyut zung	Hypothesis 假設 gaa cit
To Investigate 進行調查 jin sing diao cha	Lab Notebook 實驗室筆記本 sat yim sat bat gei bou	Laboratory 實驗室 sat yim sat[5]	Matter 物質 woe ji
Motion 運動 yuen don	Planet 星球 sing kau	Plant 植物 zik mat	Science 科學 fo hok

Math Vocabulary: Class Dictionary

To Add	Answer	To Calculate	Calculator
+	$1 + 1 = ②$	$\begin{array}{r} 7 \\ 8 \\ +5 \\ \hline 20 \end{array}$	
加	答案	計算	計算機
gaa	daap on	gai syun	gai syun gei

To Combine	To Divide	Equation	Exponent
	$\div$	$2 + 3 = 5$	A^4
組合	除	方程式	指數
git hap	ceoi	fong cing sik	zi seot

Graph	Math	To Multiply	Numbers
	3X+12	$3 \otimes 2$	$1\ 2\ 3\ 4\ 5$ $6\ 7\ 8\ 9$
圖	數學	乘	數字
tou	seot hok	sing	seot zi

To Order	Problem	Property	To Prove
$1, 2, 3, 4$	$1 + 3 = ?$	$x(y + 2)$	
整理	數學問題	數學屬性	證明
zing lei	man tai	dak sing	zing ming

To Simplify	To Solve	To Subtract	Variable
$\frac{3X + 42}{4} = 6X \longrightarrow X = 2$	$3x=12$ $X=4$	$12 \ominus 6$	x, y
簡化	解答	減	變數
gaan faa	gaai daap	gaam	bin seot

Social Studies Vocabulary: Class Dictionary

Africa	Asia	Australia	Buddhist
非洲 fei zhau	亞洲 aa zhau	澳洲 ou zhoe	佛教徒 fat gaau tou
Christian 基督徒 gei duk tou	**Citizenship** 公民身分 gong min shern fun	**Continent** 大陸 daai luk	**Country** 國家 gwok gaa
Democracy 民主 min zhoo	**Europe** 歐洲 au zhau	**Geography** 地理 dei lei	**Government** 政府 zhang foo
Hinduism 印度教 yin doo jiao	**History** 歷史 lik si	**Jewish** 猶太人 yau taai yan	**Map** 地圖 dei tou
Muslim 回教徒 muk si lam	**North American** 北美 bak mei	**South America** 北美 naam mei	**World** 世界 sai gaai

Welcome to My Classroom

Dear Parent or Guardian,

I would like to welcome your child to my classroom. The first couple of weeks can be difficult for students who don't yet speak English, but by working with you as a team I hope to make the transition as smooth as possible. While my Cantonese is not strong, I will do the best I can to communicate what is expected of your child in the classroom and in the school. Please feel free to stop by before or just after school, or to call anytime.

Again, welcome to our school! I look forward to speaking with you soon.

Sincerely,

親愛的家長或監護人：

在此歡迎貴子弟來到我的課堂。對於不會說英語的學生而言，最初的幾個星期可能有些困難。但是我希望能與您成爲一個團隊來合作，讓這個過渡期盡可能順利。 雖然我的粵語不是很流利，但是我會盡我的全力在課堂和學校與貴子弟充分 溝通。請隨時在放學前或放學後不久拜訪學校，或者隨時打電話過來。

再次歡迎您到本校來！期待能夠早日與您談話。

誠摯地，

Your Child Is a Pleasure to Have in Class

Dear Parent or Guardian,

This is a note of thanks to let you know that your child is a pleasure to have in class and to thank you for the work you do at home to help your child succeed. Though your child sometimes has difficulties with the language, he or she is trying hard and making progress every day. Keep up the good work!

Sincerely,

親愛的家長或監護人：

這是一封簡短的感謝函，目的是要讓您知道在課堂上有貴子弟令人感到無比榮幸。雖然貴子弟有時在語言上有一些困難，但是他/她非常努力，每天都在進步。希望繼續加油！

誠摯地，

Your Child Is Not Performing Up to Ability

Dear Parent or Guardian,

Though your child is smart and capable, he or she is not performing up to his or her ability. We understand that it's difficult to learn when you don't speak the language, but the only way to learn is to try, and your child needs to try harder. If you have any questions, please stop by before or just after school, or give me a call anytime.

Sincerely,

親愛的家長或監護人：

雖然貴子弟很聰明又有才華，但是並沒有發揮他/她最大的能力。我們瞭解有語言障礙時，學習將變得很困難。但是學習的唯一方法就是努力，貴子弟需要更加 努力。您若有任何問題，請隨時在放學前或放學後不久到學校來，或者隨時打電話 給我。

誠摯地,

Please Schedule a Meeting

Dear Parent or Guardian,

Please call or stop by the school office to schedule a meeting concerning your child. We understand that your time is valuable, but this is very important.

Sincerely,

親愛的家長或監護人：

請您打電話或到學校辦公室一趟，以安排一項與貴子弟有關的會議。我們知道您很繁忙，但是這件事非常重要。

誠摯地，

I am the parent of _____.

我是 _____ 的家長。.

❑ I need a translator.

❑ 我需要翻譯員。

Your Child's Behavior Is a Problem

Dear Parent or Guardian,

Your child's behavior is unacceptable. Not only does your child create an environment where he or she cannot learn, but your child is also disrupting the learning of others. I hope we can work as a team to help your child learn to behave appropriately in school. If your child continues his or her current behavior, it will result in severe disciplinary action. If you have any questions, please stop by before or just after school, or give me a call anytime.

Sincerely,

親愛的家長或監護人：

貴子弟的行爲令人無法接受。他/她不但造成一個自己無法學習的環境，還妨礙了其他學生的學習。我希望能與您成爲一個團隊來合作，以便協助貴子弟學習在學校的妥善舉止。如果貴子弟繼續他/她當前的行爲，將會導致嚴重的紀律處分。您若有任何問題，請隨時在放學前或放學後不久到學校來，或者隨時打電話給我。

誠摯地，

Absences Are Hurting Performance

Dear Parent or Guardian,

Your child's absences are hurting his or her performance. Much of what we do in school builds on what we did the day before; if a student is absent it can be very hard to catch up. I hope that we can work together as a team to help make sure that your child attends class. If you have any questions, please stop by before or just after school, or give me a call anytime.

Sincerely,

親愛的家長或監護人：

貴子弟經常曠課，嚴重影響他/她在學校的表現。我們在學校的活動有很大部分是基於我門在前一天所做的內容。如果學生曠課，他們想要趕上課程內容會很困難。但是我希望能與您成為一個團隊來合作，以確保貴子弟能夠來上課。您若有任何 問題，請隨時在放學前或放學後不久到學校來，或者隨時打電話給我。

誠摯地，

Tardiness Is Hurting Performance

Dear Parent or Guardian,

Your child is frequently late to class, and this tardiness is hurting his or her performance. By missing the beginning of the period, your child misses important directions and information, making it impossible for him or her to keep up with the rest of the class. I hope that we can work together as a team to help make sure that your child attends class. If you have any questions, please stop by before or just after school, or give me a call anytime.

Sincerely,

親愛的家長或監護人：

貴子弟上課經常遲到，這種遲到現象嚴重影響他/她在學校的表現。貴子弟若錯失課堂開始的部分，會錯失很重要的學習方向和資訊，並使他/她無法跟上班級的其他學生。我希望能與您成為一個團隊來合作，以確保貴子弟能夠準時上課。您若有任何問題，請隨時在放學前或放學後不久到學校來，或者隨時打電話給我。

誠摯地，

General Resources That School Offers

Dear Parent or Guardian,

The teachers and staff here at school hope to help you and your child in any way we can. The school offers translators and may also be able to help with school supplies and other services. Please feel free to stop by the school office anytime to explore the services available. If you work during the day, you can always call or send a note with your child. We hope to talk to you soon!

Sincerely,

親愛的家長或監護人：

本校的老師和職員都希望盡竭盡全力協助您和貴子弟。本校不但提供翻譯員服務，而且還可以在文具用品和其他服務方面為您提供協助。請隨時到學校辦公室，瞭解我們提供的各項服務。如果您在白天工作，可以打電話到學校來，或者讓貴子弟 捎帶您的便條。我們希望能夠早日與您談話！

誠摯地，

5

Korean

Kanun mari kooaya onun mari kopta

(Kind words will be met with kind words in return)

CULTURAL FACTS

Koreans in the United States

Of the more than one million Koreans living in the United States, a few are descended from early–twentieth century immigrants to Hawaii's sugar plantations, and a few immigrated during the Korean War (many as war brides), but the vast majority came to the United States after 1965, when the Immigration Act abolished the quota system that had kept numbers low. Concentrations of Korean Americans are found in Los Angeles and New York City, and in Fairfax County, VA, Bergen County, NJ, and Cook County, IL. The 2000 census found that nearly 50 percent of foreign-born Korean Americans over the age of twenty-five had earned a college degree, while 62 percent of those born in the United States had earned at least a bachelor's degree. Many Korean Americans have prospered economically and have thus assimilated to a larger degree than other immigrant groups.

The Korean Language

Korean is the official language of both North and South Korea and is also widely spoken in neighboring Yanbian, China. Korean was traditionally written using *hanja* or Chinese characters, but is now widely written using an alphabet called *hangul*, which is made up of twenty-four phonetic characters (fourteen consonants and ten vowels). South Korea continues to teach some hanja characters, while North Korea relies solely on the hangul alphabet.

Korean Religion and Culture

Korean culture and values are heavily influenced by Shamanism, Confucianism, and Buddhism (and, more recently, Christianity). The goal of much of Korean religion is to establish harmony and balance in everything (as shown by the red and blue yin-yang symbol on the Korean flag). Today, just over half of Koreans are Christians, with 40 percent of Koreans identifying themselves as one of 113 denominations of Protestant. Traditional Korean culture places an emphasis on education and respect.

Korean Holidays and Other Important Days

January 1 and 2: The *New Year's Celebration* coincides with the first day of first month of the lunar calendar.

March 1: *Independence Movement Day* commemorates the day in 1919 when Korea declared its independence from Japan.

April 5: On *Arbor Day* the Korean government encourages citizens to plant trees and other plants in response to the deforestation of the Korean War.

May 5: On *Children's Day* families visit the zoo, go to amusement parks, or participate in other entertainment.

July 17: *Constitution Day* marks the day in 1948 when the Republic of Korea unveiled its new constitution.

August 15: On *Liberation Day* in 1948, Japan surrendered to the allied forces and Korea finally gained its independence from colonial Japan.

Early October: *Cheusok,* or *The Harvest Moon Festival,* is celebrated on the fourteenth through sixteenth days of the eighth lunar month.

Pronunciation and Alphabet

Korean that is written phonetically using the Roman alphabet is pronounced as would be expected by English speakers. See the table below for a pronunciation guide for *hangul*, the Korean phonetic alphabet.

Hangul Pronunciation Guide

Consonants														
Phonetic	b, p	d, t	j	g, k	p	t	ch	k	s	h	m	n	ng	r, l
Hangul	ㅂ	ㄷ	ㅈ	ㄱ	ㅍ	ㅌ	ㅊ	ㅋ	ㅅ	ㅎ	ㅁ	ㄴ	ㅇ	ㄹ
Vowels														
Phonetic	i	a	o	u	eo	eu	ya	yo	yu	yeo				
Hangul	ㅣ	ㅏ	ㅗ	ㅜ	ㅓ	ㅡ	ㅑ	ㅛ	ㅠ	ㅕ				

Communication With Home: Useful Phrases

English	Korean Script	Pronunciation Guide
Parents	학부모	Hak-bu-mo
Mother	어머니	Eo-meo-ni
Father	아버지	Ah-beo-ji
Aunt	이모/고모	Yi-mo/go-mo
Uncle	삼촌	Samchon
Brother	형/아우/오빠/남동생	Hyong/Ah-u/Obba/Nam dongsaeng
Sister	누나/언니/여동생	Nuna/On-ni/Yeo dongsaeng
Cousin	사촌	Sachon
Boyfriend/Girlfriend	남자친구/여자친구	Namja chingu/Yeoja chingu
Whom do you live with?	누구와 함께 살아요?	Nugu-wa hamgge sa-rayo?
What is your phone number?	전화번호는 몇번이에요?	Jeonhwa beonho-nun myeot-bun-yiyeyo?
Please show this note to your ____.	이 쪽지를 ____ 에게 보여 주세요.	Yi chokji-rul ____ yege boyeo juseyo.
Please get this signed and bring it back.	여기에 서명을 하고 가져오세요.	Yeogi-ye seomyeong-ul hago gajyeo oseyo.
Please have your ____ call me at school	____ 가 학교로 내게 전화를 하도록 하세요.	____ Ga hakgyo-ro naege jeonhwa-rul hadorok haseyo.

Classroom Communication: Useful Phrases

English	Korean Script	Pronunciation Guide
Sit down please.	앉으세요.	Anju-seyo.
The assignment is on the board.	과제는 칠판 위에 적혀 있습니다.	Guajae-nun chilpan-wiye jeok-hyeo itsumnida.
Pay attention!	주의하세요!	Juyi haseyo!
Good job	잘했어요.	Jal haetseoyo.
Excellent!	아주 좋아요!	Aju jo-a-yo!
Do you need help?	도움이 필요합니까?	Do-um-yi piryo-hamnigga?
Do you understand?	을(를) 이해합니까?	Ul (rul) yihae-hamnigga?
Do you understand the assignment?	과제를 이해합니까?	Guajae-rul yihae-hamnigga?
Thanks for listening.	들어줘서 고마워요.	Deol-eo-jweo-seo gomaweoyo.
Open your book to page ____.	책 ____ 페이지를 펴세요.	Chaek ____ "page"-rul pyeo-seyo.
I know it's hard; do the best you can	힘든건 알지만 최선을 다하세요.	Him-dun-gun aljiman; choesun-ul da haseyo.
How do you say ____ in Korean?	____ 을(를) 한국말로 어떻게 말합니까?	____ ul (rul) han-gukmal-lo eo-tuk-ke malhamnigga?
What do you think about ____?	____ 에 대해서 어떻게 생각하세요?	____ -ae daehaeseo eo-tuk-ke saeng-gak haseyo?
I would like you to ____.	난 당신이 ____ 하기를 바랍니다.	Nan dangshin-yi ____ ha-gi-rul baramnida.
Do you know how to ____?	____ 을(를) 어떻게 하는지 알아요?	____ Eol (rul) eo-tuk-ke hanunji a-ra-yo?
Is this easy or hard?	쉬워요 어려워요?	Shwi-woyo eo-ryo-woyo?
Quiet, please.	조용히 하세요.	Joyonghi haseyo.
Please be careful.	조심하세요!	Joshim haseyo!

Student Communication: Useful Phrases

English	Korean Script	Pronunciation Guide
I am new.	난 새로 왔어요.	Nan saero watsumnida.
I don't speak English.	난 영어를 못해요.	Nan young-eo-rul mot-haeyo.
Do you speak ___?	당신은 ___ 를 합니까?	Dangshin-un ___ rul hamnigga?
I'm from ___.	나는 ___ 에서 왔습니다.	Nanun ___ yeseo watsumnida.
I'm sorry.	미안합니다.	Mi-an hamnida.
Excuse me.	실례합니다.	Shillae hamnida.
Thanks.	감사합니다.	Gamsa hamnida.
My name is ___.	내 이름은 ___ 입니다.	Nae yireom-eon ___ imnida.
Can you help me?	나를 도와줄 수 있습니까?	Narul dowajul-su itsumnigga?
Where is the ___?	___ 는 어디에 있습니까?	___ Nun odi-ye itsumnigga?
Can I play?	놀아도 되나요?	Nora-do doenayo?

Classroom Supplies: Class Dictionary

Book 책 chaek	Computer 컴퓨터 "computer"	Crayons 크레용 creyung	Eraser 지우개 jiwugae
Folder 폴더 "folder"	Glue 풀 pool	Markers 마커 "marker"	Note 쪽지 chok-ji
Notebook 노트북 "notebook"	Paint 페인트 "paint"	Paperclip 종이 클립 jong-yi "clip"	Pen 펜 "pen"
Pencil 연필 yeonpil	Piece of Paper 종이 jong-yi	Poster 페인트 "Poster"	Printer 프린터 "printer"
Ruler 자 ja	Scissors 가위 ga-wi	Stapler 스테이플러 "stapler"	Tape 테이프 "tape"

School Mechanics: Class Dictionary

Absent 결석 gyeolseok	Bathroom 화장실 hwa-jang-shil	Bell 벨 "bell"	Cafeteria 카페테리아 "cafeteria"
Class Period 수업 시간 su-up shigan	Clock 시계 sigae	Counselor 카운슬러 "counselor"	To Get a Drink 물 마시러 가기 mul mashireo gagi
Gymnasium 화장실 che-yuk-guan	Library 도서관 doseoguan	Locker 록커 "locker"	Lunch 점심 jeomshim
Office 교무실 gyomushil	Playground 놀이터 nol-i-toh	Principal 교장 gyojang	Recess 쉬는 시간 shwi-nun shigan
Schedule 스케줄 "schedule"	Secretary 비서 bi-seo	Tardy 지각 ji-gak	Teacher 선생님 seon-saeng-nim

Assignment Words: Class Dictionary

Assignment	Correct	Design	Directions
과제 gua-je	맞음 majeom	계획 gae-hoek	지시 ji-si
To Discuss	**To Draw**	**Due Date**	**Grade**
토론하기 to-ron hagi	그리기 gu-ri-gi	만기일 man-gi-il	성적 seong-jeok
To Help	**Homework**	**To Listen**	**Permission Letter**
도움 do-wum	숙제 suk-jae	듣기 dud-gi	허가 편지 hu-ga pyeonji
Questions	**To Read**	**Stop**	**To Take Notes**
문제 mun-jae	읽기 il-gi	읽기 jeong-ji	필기하기 pilgi-hagi
Test	**To Turn In**	**To Write**	**Wrong**
테스트 "test"	제출 jae-chul	쓰기 su-gi	틀림 tul-lim

Playground and Physical Education Vocabulary: Class Dictionary

Ball	Baseball	Basketball	To Catch
공/볼 gong	야구 ya-gu	농구 nong-gu	잡다 jab-da
To Change	Circle	Drill	Field
갈아입다 garayibda	써클 "circle"	연습 yeon-seub	운동장 un-dong-jang
To Follow	Football	Four Square	Go in Front
따르다 ta-reu-da	미식 축구 mishik chuk-gu	포 스퀘어 "four square"	앞으로 가서 ap-ero-ga-seo
Gym Clothes	Handball	To Hit	Hurt
운동복 un-dong-bok	핸드볼 "handball"	때리다 taerida	다치다 da-chi-da
To Jump	Jumprope	Kickball	Line
점프 "jump"	줄넘기 jull-num-gi	킥볼 "kickball"	줄 jool

(Continued)

(Continued)

Lock	Locker Room	To Lose	Out of Bounds
열쇠	록커 룸	지다	구역밖
yeul-shue	"locker room"	ji-da	gu-yeok-bagg
The Rules	To Run	Shoes	Sideline
규칙	달리기	신발	사이드라인
gyu-chik	dal-li-gi	shin-bahl	"sideline"
Soccer	Sport	To Stretch	Team
축구	운동	스트레치	팀
chuk-gu	un-dong	"stretch"	"team"
Tetherball	To Throw	Volleyball	Whistle
테더볼	던지기	배구	휘파람
"tetherball"	deon-ji-gi	bae-gu	hwi-pa-ram

Science Vocabulary: Class Dictionary

Acid	Animal	Base	Climate
산	동물	염기	기후
san	dong-mul	yeom-gi	gi-hu

Dinosaur	Earth	Electricity	Energy
공룡	지구	전기	에너지
gong-lyong	ji-gu	jon-gi	"energy"

Environment	Experiment	Extinct	Hypothesis
환경	실험	멸종	가설
hwan-gaeong	shil-heom	myeol-jong	ga-seol

To Investigate	Lab Notebook	Laboratory	Matter
조사하기	실험실용 노트북	실험실	물질
jo-sa-ha-gi	shil-heom-shil-yong "notebook"	shil-heom-shil	mul-jill

Motion	Planet	Plant	Science
움직임	행성	식물	과학
um-jik-im	haeng-seong	shik-mul	gua-hak

Math Vocabulary: Class Dictionary

To Add	Answer	To Calculate	Calculator
+	$1 + 1 = ②$	$\begin{array}{r} 7 \\ 8 \\ +5 \\ \hline 20 \end{array}$	
더하기	답안	계산	계산기
deo-ha-gi	dab-an	gae-san	gae-san-gi
To Combine	To Divide	Equation	Exponent
	$\div$	$2 + 3 = 5$	A^4
결합	나누기	방정식	지수
geol-hab	na-nu-gi	bang-jeong-shik	ji-su
Graph	Math	To Multiply	Numbers
		3×2	$1\ 2\ 3\ 4\ 5$ $6\ 7\ 8\ 9$
그래프	수학	곱하기	숫자
"graph"	su-hak	gob-ha-gi	sut-ja
To Order	Problem	Property	To Prove
$1, 2, 3, 4$	$1 + 3 = ?$	$x(y + 2)$	
정리하기	문제	특성	증명하기
jeong-li-ha-gi	mun-je	teuk-seong	jeung-myeong-ha-gi
To Simplify	To Solve	To Subtract	Variable
$\frac{3X + 42}{4} = 6X \longrightarrow X = 2$	$3x=12$ $X=4$	$12 - 6$	x, y
단순화하기	풀기	빼기	변수
dan-sun-hwa-ha-gi	pul-gi	pae-gi	byeon-su

Social Studies Vocabulary: Class Dictionary

Africa 아프리카 "Africa"	Asia 아시아 "Asia"	Australia 오스트레일리아 "Australia"	Buddhist 불교신자 bul-gyo-shin-ja
Christian 기독교신자 gi-dok-gyo-shin-ja	Citizenship 시민권 shi-min-gun	Continent 대륙 dae-ruk	Country 나라 na-ra
Democracy 민주주의 min-ju-ju-i	Europe 유럽 "Europe"	Geography 지리 ji-ri	Government 정부 jung-bu
Hinduism 힌두교 hin-du-gyo	History 역사 yeok-sa	Jewish 유태인 yu-tae-in	Map 지도 ji-do
Muslim 무슬림 mu-seul-lim	North American 북미 buk-mi	South America 남미 nam-mi	World 세계 sae-gae

Welcome to My Classroom

Dear Parent or Guardian,

I would like to welcome your child to my classroom. The first couple of weeks can be difficult for students who don't yet speak English, but by working with you as a team I hope to make the transition as smooth as possible. While my Korean is not strong, I will do the best I can to communicate what is expected of your child in the classroom and in the school. Please feel free to stop by before or just after school, or to call anytime.

Again, welcome to our school! I look forward to speaking with you soon.

Sincerely,

존경하는 학부모님 또는 보호자님께:

귀하의 자제분이 저의 반에 오게 된 것을 이 자리를 빌어 환영합니다. 영어를 할 줄 모르는 학생에게 있어서, 처음 몇 주는 힘들 수 있을 것입니다. 하지만 저는 이 과도기가 되도록이면 순조롭도록 귀하와 팀으로서 함께 협력하기를 바랍니다. 저의 한국어는 유창하지 않지만, 수업시간과 학교에서 귀하의 자제분과 충분히 의사소통을 할 수 있도록 최선을 다할 것입니다. 방과 전이나 방과 후 학교로 찾아오시거나 제게 언제든지 전화를 주십시오.

다시 한번 환영합니다! 귀하와 하루 빨리 대화를 나눌 수 있기를 기대합니다.

감사합니다.

Your Child Is a Pleasure to Have in Class

Dear Parent or Guardian,

This is a note of thanks to let you know that your child is a pleasure to have in class and to thank you for the work you do at home to help your child succeed. Though your child sometimes has difficulties with the language, he or she is trying hard and making progress every day. Keep up the good work!

Sincerely,

존경하는 학부모님 또는 보호자님께:

이 편지는 간단한 감사의 편지로서 저의 반에 귀하의 자제분이 온 것이 얼마나 큰 기쁨인지 말씀드리기 위해서 보내드리는 것입니다. 귀하의 자제분은 언어로 인해서 가끔 어려움도 겪지만, 아주 열심히 노력하고 있으며, 나날이 발전하고 있습니다. 계속 열심히 노력하기를 바랍니다!

감사합니다.

Your Child Is Not Performing Up to Ability

Dear Parent or Guardian,

Though your child is smart and capable, he or she is not performing up to his or her ability. We understand that it's difficult to learn when you don't speak the language, but the only way to learn is to try, and your child needs to try harder. If you have any questions, please stop by before or just after school, or give me a call anytime.

Sincerely,

존경하는 학부모님 또는 보호자님께:

귀하의 자제분은 매우 총명하고 재능도 있지만 능력을 충분히 발휘하고 있지 않습니다. 언어를 구사하지 못할 때 학습에 어려움이 있다는 것을 저희들도 이해합니다. 하지만 노력을 해야 배울 수 있는 것이며, 귀하의 자제분은 더 많은 노력을 필요로 합니다. 만약 질문이 있으시면, 방과 전이나 방과 후 학교로 찾아오시거나 제게 언제든지 전화를 주십시오.

감사합니다.

Please Schedule a Meeting

Dear Parent or Guardian,

Please call or stop by the school office to schedule a meeting concerning your child. We understand that your time is valuable, but this is very important.

Sincerely,

존경하는 학부모님 또는 보호자님께:

귀하의 자제분과 관련된 회의 일정을 정할 수 있도록 학교 교무실로 방문하시거나 전화를 해 주십시오. 귀하께서 매우 바쁘시다는 것을 저희도 알고 있지만, 이 일은 매우 중요합니다.

감사합니다.

I am the parent of _____.

아이 앰 더 패런트 오브 _____.

(나는 _____의 학부모입니다.)

❏ I need a translator.

❏ 아이 니드 어 트랜스레이터. (나는 번역인이 필요합니다.)

Your Child's Behavior Is a Problem

Dear Parent or Guardian,

Your child's behavior is unacceptable. Not only does your child create an environment where he or she cannot learn, but your child is also disrupting the learning of others. I hope we can work as a team to help your child learn to behave appropriately in school. If your child continues his or her current behavior, it will result in severe disciplinary action. If you have any questions, please stop by before or just after school, or give me a call anytime.

Sincerely,

존경하는 학부모님 또는 보호자님께:

귀하의 자제분의 행위는 용납될 수 없습니다. 귀하의 자제분은 자신의 학습 환경 뿐만 아니라, 다른 학생들의 학습 환경도 방해합니다. 저는 귀하의 자제분이 학교에서 적절한 행동을 할 수 있도록 귀하와 협력하기를 바랍니다. 만약 귀하의 자제분이 계속 그러한 행위를 할 경우 엄중한 징계 조치를 받게 될 것입니다. 만약 질문이 있으시면 방과 전이나 방과 후 학교로 찾아오시거나 제게 언제든지 전화를 주십시오.

감사합니다.

Absences Are Hurting Performance

Dear Parent or Guardian,

Your child's absences are hurting his or her performance. Much of what we do in school builds on what we did the day before; if a student is absent it can be very hard to catch up. I hope that we can work together as a team to help make sure that your child attends class. If you have any questions, please stop by before or just after school, or give me a call anytime.

Sincerely,

존경하는 학부모님 또는 보호자님께:

귀하의 자제분의 결석은 자제분의 성적에 영향을 줍니다. 저희들이 매일 학교에서 학습하는 것 중 대부분은 그 전날 한 것에 근거하기 때문에 학생이 결석을 하면 학업을 따라잡기가 매우 힘듭니다. 저는 귀하의 자제분이 수업 시간에 확실히 참여수 있도록 귀하와 협력하기를 바랍니다. 만약 질문이 있으시면 방과 전이나 방과 후 학교로 찾아오시거나 제게 언제든지 전화를 주십시오.

감사합니다.

Tardiness Is Hurting Performance

Dear Parent or Guardian,

Your child is frequently late to class, and this tardiness is hurting his or her performance. By missing the beginning of the period, your child misses important directions and information, making it impossible for him or her to keep up with the rest of the class. I hope that we can work together as a team to help make sure that your child attends class. If you have any questions, please stop by before or just after school, or give me a call anytime.

Sincerely,

존경하는 학부모님 또는 보호자님께:

귀하의 자제분이 수업 시간에 자주 지각하기 때문에 자제분의 성적에 영향을 줍니다. 수업의 시작 시간을 놓치면 중요한 지시와 정보를 놓치게 되기 때문에 수업을 따라잡기가 힘들게 됩니다. 저는 귀하의 자제분이 수업 시간에 확실히 나올 수 있도록 귀하와 함께 협력하기를 바랍니다. 만약 질문이 있으시면 언제든지 방과 전이나 방과 후 학교로 찾아오시거나 제게 전화를 주십시오.

감사합니다.

General Resources That School Offers

Dear Parent or Guardian,

The teachers and staff here at school hope to help you and your child in any way we can. The school offers translators and may also be able to help with school supplies and other services. Please feel free to stop by the school office anytime to explore the services available. If you work during the day, you can always call or send a note with your child. We hope to talk to you soon!

Sincerely,

존경하는 학부모님 또는 보호자님께:

저희 학교의 교사와 직원들은 저희들이 할 수 있는 한 모든 방법으로 귀하와 귀하의 자제분을 도와 드리고자 합니다. 저희 학교는 통역 서비스도 제공해 드리며, 학용품과 기타 서비스도 도와드릴 수 있습니다. 언제든지 학교 교무실로 오셔서 이용하실 수 있는 서비스에 대해 알아보십시오. 낮 시간에 일로 바쁘시면 언제든지 전화를 주시거나 귀하의 자제분을 통해서 편지를 보내주셔도 됩니다. 귀하와 곧 얘기를 나눌 수 있기를 바랍니다!

감사합니다.

6

Haitian Creole

Sonje lapli ki leve mayi ou

(Remember the rain that made your corn grow)

CULTURAL FACTS

Haitians in the United States

Ongoing humanitarian and political turmoil in Haiti have prompted many Haitians to seek refuge in the United States, Jamaica, the Dominican Republic, and Cuba. There are two radically different categories of Haitian immigrants—those who have applied for legal permanent resident (LPR) status, and those who have arrived illegally. The immigration rates of these two groups vary according to political events in Haiti, but they are inversely related—when the government is populist and democratic, legal immigration of the Haitian upper class soars, and when the government is military or dictatorial, the U.S. Coast Guard reports an increase in the number of Haitian refugees trying to enter the United States without documentation. For example, when the populist president Aristide has been in power, LPR immigration is high, and when there have been military coups against him, undocumented immigration has increased. Of the nearly half million people born in Haiti who now live in the United States, the majority reside in Florida or New York.

The Haitian Creole Language

Haitian Creole closely resembles French, and many residents of Haiti speak both Creole and French. However, many have considered Creole to be a lower-class language, and most Haitian literature is written in

111

French (though since the 1980s many have emphasized Creole writing in conjunction with Haitian pride). To the basis of French, Haitian Creole adds the influence of West African languages, notably Wolof, Fon, and Enwe. Despite the resemblance to French, someone speaking only French will not be able to communicate effectively with speakers of Haitian Creole. For example, while the Creole word for "good morning" (*bonjou*) closely resembles the French *bonjour*, the word for "goodbye" (*na we*) is nothing like the French *au revoir*.

Haitian Religion and Culture

Though much has been made of *Vodun*, or voodooism, Catholicism remains the country's official and dominant religion. However, while only 10 percent of Haitians practice Vodun exclusively, aspects of Vodun have made their way into Catholicism and especially into mainstream culture, and many practitioners of Vodun consider themselves Catholic. Unlike the Catholic Church, the strengthening Protestant churches (notably the Baptist, the Assemblies of God, and various evangelical denominations) do not sanction the influence of Vodun.

The cash crops of coffee, sugar, essential oils, and spices have been decimated by deforestation and the resulting loss of topsoil, as well as by the lack of economic and political stability. Subsistence fishing and farming have also suffered as sediment resulting from deforestation has smothered the surrounding coral reef systems. Though Haiti is desperately poor, it boasts a rich culture of art and music.

Haitian Holidays and Other Important Days

In addition to universal Catholic holidays, Haitian holidays include the following festivals:

January 1: *Independence Day* and *New Year's Day.*

January 2: *Ancestors' Day.*

February or March: *Carnival* takes place on the Sunday through Tuesday preceding Ash Wednesday.

May: *Mother's Day* occurs on the last Sunday in May.

October 17: *Mort de Dessalines* marks the anniversary of the death of Jean-Jacque Dessalines, considered the father (and first tyrant) of Haiti.

November 1: *All Saints Day.*

November 2: *The Day of the Dead.*

Pronunciation and Alphabet

Haitian Creole is written phonetically and each letter is pronounced. In fact, official spelling standards have been set only recently, as Haitian Creole has gained legitimacy as a national language.

Communication With Home: Useful Phrases

English	Haitian Creole	Pronunciation Guide
Parents	Paran	Par-an
Mother	Manman	Man-man
Father	Papa	Pa-pa
Aunt	Matant	Ma-tant
Uncle	Tonton	Ton-ton
Brother	Frè	Freh
Sister	Sè	Seh
Cousin	Kouzen	Kou-zen
Boyfriend/Girlfriend	Mennaj	Men-naj
Whom do you live with?	Avèk ki moun ou abite?	A-vehk ki moun ou a-bi-te?
What is your phone number?	Ki nimewo telefòn ou?	Ki ni-me-ro te-le-fohn ou?
Please show this note to your ____.	Tanpri montre ____ nòt sa a.	Tan-pri mon-tre ____ noht sa a.
Please get this signed and bring it back.	Tanpri fè yo siyen papye sa a epi pote l retounen.	Tan-pri feh yo si-yen pa-pye sa a e-pi po-te l re-tou-nen.
Please have your ____ call me at school.	Tanpri mande ____ ou pou l rele m nan lekòl la.	Tan-pri mand-de ____ ou pou l re-lem nan le-kohl la.

Classroom Communication: Useful Phrases

English	Haitian Creole	Pronunciation Guide
English	*Haitian Creole*	*Pronunciation Guide*
Sit down please.	Tanpri chita.	Tan-pri chi-ta.
The assignment is on the board.	Devwa a sou tablo a.	De-vwa a sou ta-blo a.
Pay attention!	Swiv!	Swiv!
Good job.	Bon travay.	Bon tra-vay.
Excellent!	Ekselan!	Ek-se-lan!
Do you need help?	Èske w bezwen èd?	Es-kew be-zwen ehd?
Do you understand?	Èske w konprann?	Es-kew kon-prann?
Do you understand the assignment?	Èske w konprann devwa a?	Es-kew kon-prann de-vwaa?
Thanks for listening.	Mèsi dèske w ap prete atansyon.	Meh-si dehs-ke wap pre-te a-tan-syon.
Open your book to page____.	Ouvè liv ou a nan paj____.	Ou-veh liv ou a nan paj____.
I know it's hard; do the best you can.	Mwen konnen sa pa fasil; men degaje w jan w kapab.	Mwen kon-nen sa pa fa-sil; men de-ga-jew janw ka-pab.
How do you say ____ in Haitian Creole?	Ki jan ou di ____ an kreyòl ayisyen?	Ki jan ou di ____ an kre-yohl a-yi-syen?
What do you think about ____?	Ki sa ou panse sou ____?	Ki sa ou pan-se sou ____?
I would like you to ____.	Mwen ta renmen pou ____.	Mwen ta ren-men pou ____.
Do you know how to ____?	Èske w konnen ki jan pou ____?	Es-kew kon-nen ki jan pou ____?
Is this easy or hard?	Èske sa fasil oswa difisil?	Es-ke sa fa-sil o-swa di-fi-sil?
Quiet, please.	Silans, silvouplè.	Si-lans, sil-vou-pleh.
Please be careful.	Tanpri fè atansyon.	Tan-pri feh a-tan-syon.

Student Communication: Useful Phrases

English	Haitian Creole	Pronunciation Guide
I am new.	Mwen fèk vini.	Mwen fehk vi-ni.
I don't speak English.	Mwen pa pale anglè.	Mwen pa pa-le an-gleh.
Do you speak ____?	Èske w pale ____?	Es-kew pa-leh ____?
I'm from ____.	Mwen sot ____.	Mwen sot ____.
I'm sorry.	Mwen dezole.	Mwen de-zo-leh.
Excuse me.	Eskize m.	Es-ki-zem.
Thanks.	Mèsi.	Meh-si.
My name is ____.	Mwen rele ____.	Mwen re-le ____.
Can you help me?	Èske w ka ede m?	Es-kew ka e-dem?
Where is the ____?	Ki kote m ap jwenn____?	Ki ko-te map jwenn ____.
Can I play?	Èske m ka jwe?	Es-kem ka jweh?

Classroom Supplies: Class Dictionary

Book	Computer	Crayons	Eraser
Liv	Òdinatè	Kreyon koulè	Gòm
liv	oh-di-na-teh	kre-yon kou-lè	gohm
Folder	Glue	Markers	Note
Dosye	Lakòl	Makè	Nòt
do-sye	la-kol	ma-keh	noht
Notebook	Paint	Paperclip	Pen
Kaye	Penti	Agrafez	Plim
ka-ye	pen-ti	a-gra-fez	plim
Pencil	Piece of Paper	Poster	Printer
Kreyon	Moso papye	Postè	Enprimant
kre-yon	mo-so pa-pye	pos-teh	en-pri-mant
Ruler	Scissors	Stapler	Tape
Règ	Sizo	Agrafèz	Tep
rehg	si-zo	a-gra-fehz	teip

School Mechanics: Class Dictionary

Absent Absan ab-san	Bathroom Twalèt twa-leht	Bell Klòch klohch	Cafeteria Kafeterya ka-fe-te-rya
Class Period È ansèyman eh an-sehy-man	Clock Òlòj oh-lohj	Counselor Konseye kon-se-ye	To Get a Drink Pran yon bagay pou bwè pran yon ba-gay pou bweh
Gymnasium Jimnazyòm jim-na-zyohm	Library Bibliyotèk bi-bli-yo-tehk	Locker Kazye ka-zye	Lunch Lench lench
Office Biwo bi-wo	Playground Teren Jwet te-ren jwet	Principal Direktè di-rek-teh	Recess Rekreyasyon re-kre-ya-syon
Schedule Orè o-reh	Secretary Sekretè se-kre-teh	Tardy Anreta an-re-ta	Teacher Pwofesè pwo-fe-seh

Assignment Words: Class Dictionary

Assignment	Correct	Design	Directions
Devwa	Kòrèk	Plan	Enstriksyon
de-vwah	koh-rehk	plan	ens-trik-syon
To Discuss	To Draw	Due Date	Grade
Diskite	Desine	Dat pou remèt devwa	Nòt
dis-ki-teh	de-si-ne	dat pou re-meht de-vwah	noht
To Help	Homework	To Listen	Permission Letter
Ede	Devwa pou fè lakay	Koute	Lèt pou mande pèmisyon
e-de	de-vwah pou feh la-kay	kou-teh	leht pou man-de peh-mi-syon
Questions	To Read	Stop	To Take Notes
Kesyon	Li	Kanpe	Pran nòt
ke-syon	lee	kan-pe	pran-noht
Test	To Turn In	To Write	Wrong
Egzamen	Remèt devwa	Ekri	Pa kòrèk
eg-za-men	re-meht de-vwah	eh-kree	pa-koh-rehk

Playground and Physical Education Vocabulary: Class Dictionary

Ball Balon ba-lon	Baseball Bezbòl bez-bohl	Basketball Baskètbòl bas-keht-bohl	To Catch Trape tra-pe
To Change Chanje chan-je	Circle Sèk sek	Drill Egzèse eg-zeh-se	Field Teren te-ren
To Follow Swiv swiv	Football (American) Foutbòl ameriken fout-bohl am-er-ee-kehn	Four Square Kat Kare kat ka-re	Go in Front Ale Devan a-le de-van
Gym Clothes Rad jimnastik rad jim-nas-tik	Handball Boul voye ak men bul vo-ye ak men	To Hit Frape fra-pe	Hurt Blese ble-se
To Jump Sote so-te	Jumprope Sote kòd so-te kod	Kickball Boul voye ak pye bul vo-ye ak pije	Line Liy liy

(Continued)

(Continued)

Lock Kadna kad-na	Locker Room Sal kazye sal ka-zye	To Lose Pèdi peh-di	Out of Bounds Andeyò limit an-de-yoh li-mit
The Rules RULES The ckoskd cldlj ekd ckdou. Kndk dui idu nduy. Liehy djsulkll giehd ckdlly clidusk ldicljy djywo dlclsdj bldinueodk cldlin uey Ecly dlihdyope. giehd ckdlly clidusk Règ yo rehg-yo	To Run Kouri kou-ri	Shoes Soulye sou-lye	Sideline Limit teren an li-mit te-ren
Soccer Foutbòl fout-bohl	Sport Espò es-poh	To Stretch Detire de-tir-e	Team Ekip e-kip
Tetherball Boul Long boul long	To Throw Voye vo-ye	Volleyball Volebòl vo-le-bohl	Whistle Siflèt si-fleht

Science Vocabulary: Class Dictionary

Acid	Animal	Base	Climate
Asid	Bèt	Baz	Klima
a-sid	beht	baz	kli-mah
Dinosaur	Earth	Electricity	Energy
Dinozò	Latè	Elektwisite	Enèji
di-no-zoh	la-tè	e-lek-tri-si-te	e-neh-ji
Environment	Experiment	Extinct	Hypothesis
Anviwonnman	Eksperyans	Ekstèmine	Ipotèz
an-vi-won-man	eks-pe-ryans	eks-teh-mi-ne	i-po-tehz
To Investigate	Lab Notebook	Laboratory	Matter
Envestige	Kaye laboratwa	Laboratwa	Matyè
en-ves-ti-ge	ka-ye la-bo-ra-twah	la-bo-ra-twah	ma-tyè
Motion	Planet	Plant	Science
Mouvman	Planèt	Plant	Syans
mouv-man	pla-neht	plant	syans

Math Vocabulary: Class Dictionary

To Add	Answer	To Calculate	Calculator
Adisyone	Repons	Kalkile	Kalkilatris
a-di-syo-ne	re-pons	kal-ki-le	kal-ki-la-tris
To Combine	**To Divide**	**Equation**	**Exponent**
Konbine	Divize	Ekwasyon	ekspozan
kon-bi-ne	di-vi-ze	e-kwa-syon	eks-po-zan
Graph	**Math**	**To Multiply**	**Numbers**
Grafik	Matematik	Miltipliye	Chif
gra-fik	ma-te-ma-tik	mil-ti-pli-ye	chif
To Order	**Problem**	**Property**	**To Prove**
Mete nan lòd	Pwoblèm	Pwopriyete	Pwouve
me-te nan lohd	pwo-blehm	pwo-pri-ye-te	pwou-ve
To Simplify	**To Solve**	**To Subtract**	**Variable**
Senplifye	Rezoud	Soustrè	Varyab
sen-pli-fye	re-zoud	sous-treh	va-ryab

To Calculate:
$$\begin{array}{r} 7 \\ 8 \\ +5 \\ \hline 20 \end{array}$$

Answer: $1 + 1 = 2$

Equation: $2 + 3 = 5$

Exponent: A^4

To Multiply: 3×2

Numbers: $1\ 2\ 3\ 4\ 5\ 6\ 7\ 8\ 9$

To Order: $1, 2, 3, 4$

Problem: $1 + 3 = ?$

Property: $x(y + 2)$

To Simplify: $\frac{3X + 42}{4} = 6X \longrightarrow X = 2$

To Solve: $3x = 12$, $X = 4$

To Subtract: $12 - 6$

Variable: x, y

Social Studies Vocabulary: Class Dictionary

Africa	Asia	Australia	Buddhist
Afrik	Azi	Ostrali	Boudis
a-frik	a-zee	os-tra-li	bou-dis
Christian	Citizenship	Continent	Country
Kretyen	Sitwayènte	Kontinan	Peyi
kre-tyen	si-twa-yen-te	kon-ti-nan	pe-yee
Democracy	Europe	Geography	Government
Demokrasi	Ewòp	Jeyografi	Gouvènman
de-mo-kra-si	e-wohp	je-yo-gra-fee	gou-ven-man
Hinduism	History	Jewish	Map
Indouism	Istwa	Jwif	Kat jeyografik
en-dou-yism	is-twa	jwif	kat je-wo-gra-fik
Muslim	North American	South America	World
Mizilman	Amerik dinò	Amerik disid	Lemonn
mi-zil-man	a-me-rik di-noh	a-me-rik di-sid	le-mon

Welcome to My Classroom

Dear Parent or Guardian,

I would like to welcome your child to my classroom. The first couple of weeks can be difficult for students who don't yet speak English, but by working with you as a team I hope to make the transition as smooth as possible. While my Haitian Creole is not strong, I will do the best I can to communicate what is expected of your child in the classroom and in the school. Please feel free to stop by before or just after school, or to call anytime.

Again, welcome to our school! I look forward to speaking with you soon.

Sincerely,

Chè paran oswa gadyen,

Mwen ta renmen akeyi pitit ou a nan klas mwen an. Premye semèn yo ka difisil pou elèv ki poko ka pale anglè, men lè nou travay ansanm tankou yon ekip mwen espere leplis posib fasilite tranzisyon an. Byenke kreyòl mwen pa twò fò, mwen pral fè tout sa m kapab pou m kominike ki sa nou atann de pitit ou an nan klas la ak nan lekòl la. Tanpri santi w alèz pou pase anvan oswa imedyatman aprè lekòl la, oswa ou ka rele m nenpòt lè.

Ankò, byenveni nan lekòl nou an ! Mwen espere pale avèk ou trè byento.

Sensèman,

Your Child Is a Pleasure to Have in Class

Dear Parent or Guardian,

This is a note of thanks to let you know that your child is a pleasure to have in class and to thank you for the work you do at home to help your child succeed. Though your child sometimes has difficulties with the language, he or she is trying hard and making progress every day. Keep up the good work!

Sincerely,

Chè paran oswa gadyen,

Sa se yon nòt remèsiman pou fè w konnen se yon plezi pou m genyen elèv ou a nan klas mwen an. Byenke elèv ou an pafwa gen difikilte ak lang lan, l ap fè anpil efò epi l ap fè anpil pwogrè chak jou. Kontinye fè bon travay !

Sensèman,

Your Child Is Not Performing Up to Ability

Dear Parent or Guardian,

Though your child is smart and capable, he or she is not performing up to his or her ability. We understand that it's difficult to learn when you don't speak the language, but the only way to learn is to try, and your child needs to try harder. If you have any questions, please stop by before or just after school, or give me a call anytime.

Sincerely,

Chè paran oswa gadyen,

Byenke elèv ou a fò epi li kapab, li pa fè tout efò li te ka fè selon kapasite li. Nou konprann li difisil pou aprann lè w pa pale lang lan, men sèl fason pou aprann se lè w eseye epi elèv ou an bezwen eseye plis. Si w ta gen nenpòt kesyon, tanpri pase anvan oswa imedyatman aprè lekòl la, oswa ou ka rele m nenpòt lè.

Sensèman,

Please Schedule a Meeting

Dear Parent or Guardian,

Please call or stop by the school office to schedule a meeting concerning your child. We understand that your time is valuable, but this is very important.

Sincerely,

Chè paran oswa gadyen,

Tanpri rele oswa pase nan biwo lekòl la pou pwograme yon randevou konsènan elèv ou an. Nou konprann tan ou presye, men sa se yon bagay ki enpòtan anpil.

Sensèman,

I am the parent of _____.

Mwen se paran _____.

❑ I need a translator.

❑ Mwen bezwen yon entèprèt.

Your Child's Behavior Is a Problem

Dear Parent or Guardian,

Your child's behavior is unacceptable. Not only does your child create an environment where he or she cannot learn, but your child is also disrupting the learning of others. I hope we can work as a team to help your child learn to behave appropriately in school. If your child continues his or her current behavior, it will result in severe disciplinary action. If you have any questions, please stop by before or just after school, or give me a call anytime.

Sincerely,

Chè paran oswa gadyen,

Konpòtman elèv ou an pa akseptab. Non sèlman li kreye yon anviwonman kote li paka aprann, men tou li deranje lòt yo k ap eseye aprann. Mwen espere nou ka travay kòm yon ekip pou ede elèv ou an aprann konpòte l de fason apwopriye nan lekòl la. Si elèv ou an kontinye ak menm konpòtman sa a, li pral sibi aksyon disiplinè ki sevè. Si w ta gen nenpòt kesyon tanpri pase anvan oswa imedyatman aprè lekòl la, oswa rele m nenpòt lè.

Sensèman,

Absences Are Hurting Performance

Dear Parent or Guardian,

Your child's absences are hurting his or her performance. Much of what we do in school builds on what we did the day before; if a student is absent it can be very hard to catch up. I hope that we can work together as a team to help make sure that your child attends class. If you have any questions, please stop by before or just after school, or give me a call anytime.

Sincerely,

Chè paran oswa gadyen,

Absans elèv ou a nan lekòl la ap afekte pèfòmans li. Pifò nan sa nou fè lekòl la bati sou sa nou te fè jou avan an ; si yon elèv absan li ka difisil anpil pou l ratrape li. Mwen espere nou ka travay ansanm kòm yon ekip pou ede asire elèv ou an vini lekòl. Si w ta gen nenpòt kesyon tanpri pase anvan oswa imedyatman aprè lekòl la, oswa rele m nenpòt lè.

Sensèman,

Tardiness Is Hurting Performance

Dear Parent or Guardian,

Your child is frequently late to class, and this tardiness is hurting his or her performance. By missing the beginning of the period, your child misses important directions and information, making it impossible for him or her to keep up with the rest of the class. I hope that we can work together as a team to help make sure that your child attends class. If you have any questions, please stop by before or just after school, or give me a call anytime.

Sincerely,

Chè paran oswa gadyen,

Elèv ou an souvan anreta nan klas la, epi reta sa a ap afekte pèfòmans li. Lè elèv ou an manke kòmansman peryòd la, li rate enstriksyon ak enfòmasyon enpòtan, sa ki vin fè li enposib pou li rete nan menm nivo ak rès klas la. Mwen espere nou ka travay ansanm kòm yon ekip pou asire elèv ou an vini lekòl. Si w ta gen nenpòt kesyon tanpri pase anvan oswa imedyatman aprè lekòl la, oswa rele m nenpòt lè.

Sensèman,

General Resources That School Offers

Dear Parent or Guardian,

The teachers and staff here at school hope to help you and your child in any way we can. The school offers translators and may also be able to help with school supplies and other services. Please feel free to stop by the school office anytime to explore the services available. If you work during the day, you can always call or send a note with your child. We hope to talk to you soon!

Sincerely,

Chè paran oswa gadyen,

Pwofesè yo ak pèsonèl la nan lekòl la vle ede w ansanm ak elèv ou a nan tout fason nou kapab. Lekòl la ofri tradiktè epi li posib yo ka ede w tou ak materyèl pou lekòl la ak lòt sèvis tou. Tanpri santi w alèz pou pase nan biwo lekòl la nenpòt lè pou dekouvri sèvis ki disponib yo. Si w travay pandan lajounen, ou ka toujou rele oswa voye yon nòt avèk elèv ou an. Nou espere pale avèk ou byento !

Sensèman,

7

Arabic

اعمل الطيب وارمه البحر

E'mal ettayeb warmehi fel bahr

*(Do a good deed and throw it in the sea
[or, a good deed is a reward in itself])*

CULTURAL FACTS

Arabic Speakers in the United States

The speakers of Arabic in the United States are a relatively diverse group, coming from many countries throughout the Middle East and North Africa. The 2000 census found that people of Arab descent living in the United States earned more money per capita than the general population and were more likely to be educated. However, a higher portion of people of Arab descent also lived below the poverty line (17 percent versus 12 percent). Of the 850,000 people who reported Arab ancestry alone, nearly three-quarters spoke English "very well." This is one of the most quickly growing populations in the United States, having increased 40 percent during the 1990s alone.

The Arabic Language

As would be expected for a language spoken in such a wide geographic area and across so many national boundaries, many dialects of Arabic exist. The two primary dialect groups are those spoken in North Africa (the *Al-Maghreb Al-Arabi*), and those spoken in Middle Eastern

133

countries. Speakers of Arabic from the Middle East can generally understand one another, despite regional variations, but they may not be able to understand Arabic speakers from North Africa. North Africans, however, usually understand speech from the Middle East, due to the popularity of Egyptian films.

Arabic Religion and Culture

While Arabic culture is rather diverse across national boundaries, the religion of the Arabic world is almost universally Islam. Traditionally, the Arabic-speaking world has been rich in poetry, calligraphy, architecture, and painting.

Holidays and Other Important Days of the Arabic-Speaking World

The Islamic year (called the *Al-Sana Al-Hijria*) is based on the lunar year, rather than the solar year, and is thus 354 days long. Check the Internet for the Gregorian calendar dates of this year's festivals. While each Arabic-speaking country celebrates its own national holidays, the Muslim world generally celebrates the following Islamic holidays:

Hijrah: The New Year.

Milad-e Nabi Mawlid an Nabi: The birthday of the Prophet Muhammad.

Laylat al-Mi'raj: Celebration marking the ascent of the Prophet Muhammad to God.

Ramadan: The month of fasting during which Muslim people do not eat or drink between sunrise and sunset.

Layla tul Qadr: Known as the Night of Destiny, this holiday takes place during Ramadan and is marked by all-night prayer.

Eid al Fitr: This feast marks the end of Ramadan.

Eid al Adha: These celebrations in remembrance of the sacrifice of the Prophet Abraham last for four days.

Pronunciation and Alphabet

There are two major systems for representing Arabic using the Roman alphabet. Recreating the sounds of Arabic exactly requires many diacritics, while the common method uses consonant blends (such as sh and kh) that only approximate Arabic sounds, but are much easier to read. The Modern Standard Arabic Alphabet itself contains twenty-eight letters, shown in the table on the following page with their phonetic transcriptions. Unlike English, Arabic script is read from right to left.

The Modern Standard Arabic Alphabet, With Phonetic Translations

ا	ب	ت	ث	ج	ح	خ	د	ذ	ر	ز	س	ش	ص
a	b	t	th	j	h	kh	d	dh	r	z	s	sh	s

ض	ط	ظ	ع	غ	ف	ق	ك	ل	م	ن	ه	و	ي
d	t	z/dh	(break)	g, gh	f	q	k	l	m	n	h	w, u	y, i

Communication With Home: Useful Phrases

English	Arabic Script	Pronunciation
Parents	الوالدين	Al-wali-dayn
Mother	أم	'Um
Father	أب	Ab
Aunt	عمة / خالة	Ammah / Khala
Uncle	عم / خال	Am/ Khal
Brother	أخ	A'kh
Sister	أخت	U-kht
Cousin	إبن العم / إبن الخال	Ibn-al-am / Ibn-al-khal
Boyfriend/Girlfriend	صديقي / صديقتي	Sadi-qee/Sadi-qa-ti
Whom do you live with?	مع من انت تعيش؟	M'a men ta eesh?
What is your phone number?	ماهو رقم تليفونك؟	Ma howa Raqam telephoneqa?
Please show this note to your ____.	من فضلك اعرض هذه المذآرة على ____.	Min fad-lak e'a-rid al-warqa 'ala____.
Please get this signed and and bring it back.	من فضلك دع أحد يوقع واحضرها لي.	Min fad-lak da'a ahad yuwaqi' wa ah-diriha li.
Please have your ____ call me at school.	المدرسة من فضلك دع ____ ك يخابرني في	Min-fad-lak da'a ____ yi-khabir-ni fil-mad-rasah.

Classroom Communication: Useful Phrases

English	Arabic Script	Pronunciation
Sit down, please.	إجلس من فضلك.	Ej-lis min, fad-lak.
The assignment is on the board.	المهمة مكتوبة على السبورة.	Al-mu-him-mah mak-tooba-'ala al-sab-boo-rah.
Pay attention!	انتبه!	In-tabeh!
Good job.	عملٌ جيدٌ!	'Amel jayid.
Excellent!	ممتاز!	Mum-taz!
Do you need help?	تحتاج اي مساعدة؟	Hel tih-taj iy mos'a-dah?
Do you understand?	هل تفهم؟	Hel taf-ham?
Do you understand the assignment?	هل تفهم المهمة؟	Hel taf-ham al-mo-him-mah?
Thanks for listening.	شكراً للاستماع.	Shuk-ran lil-istima'.
Open your book to page ____.	افتح كتابك على صفحة ـــــ.	Eftah kita-bak saf-ha ____.
I know it's hard; do the best you can.	انا اعلم انه صعب ، افعل مافي استطاعتك.	Ana 'alam enno sa'ab ef'al ma-fi isti-t'a-atak.
How do you say ____ in Arabic?	كيف تقول ـــــ بالعربي؟	Kayf taq-ol ____ in Arabi?
What do you think about ____?	ماهو رأيك في ـــــ؟	Ma howa r'yak fi ____?
I would like you to ____.	أريدك أن ـــــ.	Oridooka an ____.
Do you know how to ____?	هل تعرف كيف ـــــ؟	Hel ta'arf kayf ____?
Is this easy or hard?	هل هذا سهل أم صعب؟	Hel haza sahil am sa'ab?
Quiet, please.	هدوء من فضلك.	Hudo' min fad-lak.
Please be careful.	كن حذر.	Kun ha-thir.

Student Communication: Useful Phrases

English	Arabic Script	Pronunciation
I am new.	أنا جديد.	Ana ja-deed.
I don't speak English.	لا أتكلم انجليزي.	Ana la ata-ka-lam En-gli-zee.
Do you speak ____?	هل تتكلم ____؟	Hal tata-ka-lam ____?
I'm from ____.	أنا من ____.	Ana min ____.
I'm sorry.	أنا آسف.	Ana asif.
Excuse me.	لو سمحت.	Law sa-maht.
Thanks.	شكراً.	Shuk-ran.
My name is ____.	إسمي ____.	'Is-mee ____.
Can you help me?	ممكن تساعدني؟	Mom-kin tsa-'ad-nee?
Where is the ____?	أين ال ____؟	Ayna al ____?
Can I play?	ممكن العب ؟	Mom-kin 'al-'ab?

Classroom Supplies: Class Dictionary

Book	Computer	Crayons	Eraser
كتاب ki-tab	كمبيوتر comb-you-tar	أقلام تلوين aq-laam tal-ween	ممسحة mam-saha
Folder	**Glue**	**Markers**	**Note**
ملف مدرسي ma-laf mad-rasee	غِراء ghi-raa'	قلم الوان qa-lam al-wan	مذكرة mu-zakka-rah
Notebook	**Paint**	**Paperclip**	**Pen**
كراسة kur-rasah	هان di-han	دبوس ورق da-bous waraq	قلم qalam
Pencil	**Piece of Paper**	**Poster**	**Printer**
قلم رصاص qalam rasas	قطعة من الورق wara-ka	لائحة la-ehah	طابعة كمبيوتر tabi-'ah
Ruler	**Scissors**	**Stapler**	**Tape**
مسطرة mas-ta-ra	مقص ma-qass	دباسة dab-ba-sah	شَريط sha-reet

School Mechanics: Class Dictionary

Absent غائب gha-yib	Bathroom حمام ham-mam	Bell جرس المدرسة ja-ras al-mad-ra-sah	Cafeteria كافيتريا kafi-ter-yah
Class Period الفترة الدراسية al-fat-ra al-dera-sayah	Clock ساعة حائط sa'at ha-it	Counselor مشرف المدرسة mush-rif mad-ra-sah	To Get a Drink يحضر شراب yuh-dir sha-rab
Gymnasium الملعب الرياضي al-mal-'ab al-re-ya-dee	Library مكتبة mak-ta-bah	Locker دولاب dou-lab	Lunch غداء gha-da
Office مكتب mak-tab	Playground مَلعب mal-'ab	Principal ناظر / ناظرة na-zir/ na-zir-rah	Recess أبحاث ab-hath
Schedule 8:30 Welcome/Class Business 9:00 Language Arts 10:30 Mathematics 11:30 Social Studies 12:00 Lunch 1:00 Science 2:00 Art/Music/PE جدول jad-wal	Secretary سكرتير / سكرتيرة si-kir-teer / si-kir-tee-ra	Tardy متأخر على الفصل mit-'akhr 'an al-fasl	Teacher مدرس / مدرسة mu-dar-ris / mu-dar-ri-sa

Assignment Words: Class Dictionary

Assignment مهمة mu-him-mah	Correct صحيح sa-heeh	Design تصميم yu-khat-tet	Directions توجيهات (ارشادات الواجب) ir-sha-dat (ir-sha-dat al-wa-jeb)
To Discuss يناقش yu-na-qish	To Draw يرسم yar-sim	Due Date آخر ميعاد a-khir mi-'ad	Grade درجات da-ra-jat
To Help يساعد yu-sa-'aid	Homework واجب wa-jib	To Listen يسمع yas-ma'	Permission Letter ورقة اذن wa-ra-kat ez-in
Questions أسئلة as-eh-lah	To Read يقرأ ya-qra'	Stop قف qif	To Take Notes يلخص yu-lakh-'es
Test إمتحان em-te-han	To Turn In تسليم الواجب tas-leem al-wa-jib	To Write يكتب yak-tib	Wrong خطأ kha-ta'

Playground and Physical Education Vocabulary: Class Dictionary

Ball	Baseball	Basketball	To Catch
كرة ku-rah	كرة البيسبول ku-rat al-bis-bool	كرة السلة ku-rat al-sal-lah	يمسك yam-sik
To Change	Circle	Drill	Field
يغير yu-gha-yir	دائرة da-e-rah	تمرين taj-re-bah	ملعب mal-'ab
To Follow	Football (American)	Four Square	Go in Front
يتبع yat'ba'	match kurah	mu-rab-ba'a	إنطلق في المقدمة in-ta-leq fil-mu-qad-dima
Gym Clothes	Handball	To Hit	Hurt
الملابس الرياضية al- mal-bis al-re-ya-dy-yah	كرة اليَد ku-rat al-yadd	يضرب ya-dreb	وجع wa-j'a
To Jump	Jumprope	Kickball	Line
يقفز yaq-fiz	حَبل القفز habl al-qafz	كُرة الرَكل ku-rat ar-rakl	صف saf

Lock قفل qifil	Locker Room حجرة تغيير الملابس ho-j-rah al-ma-la-bis	To Lose يخسر kha-ser	Out of Bounds خارج الخط kha-rij el-khat
The Rules القواعد al-qwa-'id	To Run يجري yaj-ree	Shoes أحذية ah-zyya	Sideline الخط الجانبي khat had al-mal-'ab
Soccer كرة قدم kurat qa-dam	Sport رياضة re-ya-dah	To Stretch يسترخي yas-tar-khee	Team فريق fa-reeq
Tetherball كُرة الطِوَل ku-rat at-ti-wal	To Throw يرمي yar-me	Volleyball الكرة الطائرة al-kurah al-ta-yirah	Whistle صفارة sof-fa-rah

Science Vocabulary: Class Dictionary

Acid حامض ha-mid	Animal حيوان haya-wan	Base قلوي qa-la-wee	Climate طقس taq-s
Dinosaur ديناصور die-na-soor	Earth أرض ard	Electricity كهرباء kah-ra-baa'	Energy نشاط na-shat
Environment بيئة bee'ah	Experiment تجربة taj-ri-bah	Extinct منقرض mon-qa-red	Hypothesis فرضيات fara-day-yat
To Investigate يُحقق في yu-haq-qeq fee	Lab Notebook كراسة مختبر ku-ra-sit m'a-mal	Laboratory مختبر ma'a-mal	Matter مادّة maa-dda
Motion حَركة ha-ra-ka	Planet كوكب kaw-kab	Plant زرع zar-'a	Science علوم o-loom

Math Vocabulary: Class Dictionary

To Add	Answer	To Calculate	Calculator
$+$	$1 + 1 = ②$	$\begin{array}{r} 7 \\ 8 \\ +5 \\ \hline 20 \end{array}$	
يجمع	جواب	يحسب	آلة حاسبة
ya-jm'a	jawab	yah-seb	alah has-bah

To Combine	To Divide	Equation	Exponent
	$\div$	$2 + 3 = 5$	A^4
يجمع بين	يقسم	معادلة	الأسية
daj-m'a bayn	yu qa-sim	mu 'ad-lah	al-o-sy-yah

Graph	Math	To Multiply	Numbers
		$3 \otimes 2$	$\begin{array}{l} 1\ 2\ 3\ 4\ 5 \\ 6\ 7\ 8\ 9 \end{array}$
رسم بياني	حساب	يضرب	أرقام
ra-sim ba-ya-ni	he-sab	darb	ar-qam

To Order	Problem	Property	To Prove
$1, 2, 3, 4$	$1 + 3 = ?$	$x(y + 2)$	
ينظم	مسألة	رمز جبري	يبرهن
yu-na-zim	mas-'alah	ramz jab-ri	yu-bar-hin

To Simplify	To Solve	To Subtract	Variable
$\frac{3X + 42}{4} = 6X \longrightarrow X = 2$	$\begin{array}{l} 3x=12 \\ X=4 \end{array}$	$12 \ominus 6$	x, y
يبسط	يحل	يطرح	المتغيرات
yu-ba-sit	yu-hil	yun-qis	al-mu-ta-ghy-ya-rat

Social Studies Vocabulary: Class Dictionary

Africa أفريقيا af-reeq-ya	Asia آسيا a-sya	Australia أستراليا ust-ral-ya	Buddhist بوذي bou-zee
Christian مسيحي masee-hee	Citizenship جنسية mu-waa-ti-niy-ya	Continent قارة qa-rah	Country دولة daw-lah
Democracy ديمقر اطيّة di-moq-raa-tiy-ya	Europe أوربا aw-ro-ba	Geography جغرافيا jo-gh-ra-fya	Government حُكومة hou-kou-ma
Hinduism هِندوسيّة hin-dou-siy-ya	History تاريخ ta-reekh	Jewish يهود ي ya-hood	Map خريطة kha-ri-tah
Muslim مسلم mus-lim	North American امريكا الشمالية am-ree-ka al-sha-ma-ly-yah	South America امريكا الجنوبية am-ree-ka al-ja-no-by-yah	World العالم al-'a-lam

Welcome to My Classroom

Dear Parent or Guardian,

I would like to welcome your child to my classroom. The first couple of weeks can be difficult for students who don't yet speak English, but by working with you as a team I hope to make the transition as smooth as possible. While my Arabic is not strong, I will do the best I can to communicate what is expected of your child in the classroom and in the school. Please feel free to stop by before or just after school, or to call anytime.

Again, welcome to our school! I look forward to speaking with you soon.

Sincerely,

عزيزي ولي الأمر،

أحب أن أرحب بطفلك في فصلي. قد تكون ألاسابيع الأولى صعبة علي الطلاب الذين لا يتكلمون الانجليزية. ولكنني أأمل بأننا إذا عملنا معاً كفريق واحد سنستطيع أن نجعل مرحلة الانتقال سلسة وسهلة. وبالرغم من أن لغتي العربية ليست ممتازة ولكني سأبذل قصارى جهدي لأيصال ماهو مطلوب من طفلك في الفصل وفي المدرسة اليك. تفضل بالحضور قبل أو بعد فترة الدراسة مباشرةً او يمكنك مخابرتي في أي وقت تشاء.

أرحب بكم مرة أخرى في مدرستنا! أتمنى أن أتكلم معك قريباً.

المخلص،

Your Child Is a Pleasure to Have in Class

Dear Parent or Guardian,

This is a note of thanks to let you know that your child is a pleasure to have in class and to thank you for the work you do at home to help your child succeed. Though your child sometimes has difficulties with the language, he or she is trying hard and making progress every day. Keep up the good work!

Sincerely,

عزيزي ولي الأمر
هذه مذكرة شكر لإعلامك بأننا مسرورون بوجود طفلك في الفصل. ونشكرك كذلك على الجهود التي تقوم بها في البيت لتساعد طفلك على النجاح. و بالرغم من أن طفلك مازالت لديه صعوبات في اللغة فهو/ هي يحاول / تحاول كثيراً ويتقدم / تتقدم كل يوم. داوم على العمل الجيد!
المخلص،

Your Child Is Not Performing Up to Ability

Dear Parent or Guardian,

Though your child is smart and capable, he or she is not performing up to his or her ability. We understand that it's difficult to learn when you don't speak the language, but the only way to learn is to try, and your child needs to try harder. If you have any questions, please stop by before or just after school, or give me a call anytime.

Sincerely,

عزيزي ولي الأمر،

بالرغم من ان تلميذك ذكي ومقتدر، فإن أداءه / أداءها لا يعادل قدراته / قدراتها. نحن نعلم أنه من الصعب أن تتعلم وانت لا تتكلم اللغة، ولكن الطريقة الوحيدة للتعلم هي أن تثابر، وتلميذك محتاج أن يحاول ويثابر أكثر. إذا كانت لديك أية أسئلة فأرجو أن تحضر قبل أو بعد فترة الدراسة، أو الإتصال بي هاتفياً في أي وقت تشاء.

المخلص،

Please Schedule a Meeting

Dear Parent or Guardian,

Please call or stop by the school office to schedule a meeting concerning your child. We understand that your time is valuable, but this is very important.

Sincerely,

عزيزي ولي الأمر،

نرجو منك الإتصال بنا هاتفياً أو الحضور الى مكتبنا في المدرسة لتحديد موعد للإجتماع بخصوص طفلك.

نحن نعلم أن وقتك ثمين، ولكن هذا الاجتماع ضروري جداً.

المخلص،

I am the parent of _____.

_____ مر

☐   I need a translator.

☐ أنا بحاجة لمترجم

Your Child's Behavior Is a Problem

Dear Parent or Guardian,

Your child's behavior is unacceptable. Not only does your child create an environment where he or she cannot learn, but your child is also disrupting the learning of others. I hope we can work as a team to help your child learn to behave appropriately in school. If your child continues his or her current behavior, it will result in severe disciplinary action. If you have any questions, please stop by before or just after school, or give me a call anytime.

Sincerely,

عزيزي ولي الأمر،

سلوك تلميذك غير مقبول. أنه / أنها لايخلق بيئة يصعب التعلم فيها فحسب، بل إنه / إنها يعطل عملية التعليم للآخرين أيضاً. آمل أن نستطيع العمل معاً كفريق واحد لكي نساعد تلميذك على أن يتصرف بشكل مناسب في المدرسة. إذا إستمر تلميذك في سلوكه / سلوكها الحالي، فسوف ينتج هذا إتخاذ إجراء إنضباطي صارم بحقه. إذا كانت لديك أية أسئلة فأرجو أن تحضر قبل أو بعد فترة الدراسة، أو الإتصال بي هاتفياً في أي وقت تشاء.

المخلص،

Absences Are Hurting Performance

Dear Parent or Guardian,

Your child's absences are hurting his or her performance. Much of what we do in school builds on what we did the day before; if a student is absent it can be very hard to catch up. I hope that we can work together as a team to help make sure that your child attends class. If you have any questions, please stop by before or just after school, or give me a call anytime.

Sincerely,

عزيزي ولي الأمر،

إن غياب تلميذك سوف يضر بأداءه / أداءها . إن الكثير مما ننجزه في المدرسة يعتمد على ما انجزناه في اليوم السابق .فإذا تغيب الطالب، فسوف يكون صعباً عليه أن يلحق بالفصل .وآمل أن نستطيع العمل معاً كفريق واحد لكي نساعد تلميذك على أن يواظب في حضوره الى الفصل. إذا كانت لديك أية أسئلة فأرجو أن تحضر قبل أو بعد فترة الدراسة، أو الإتصال بي هاتفياً في أي وقت تشاء.

المخلص،

Tardiness Is Hurting Performance

Dear Parent or Guardian,

Your child is frequently late to class, and this tardiness is hurting his or her performance. By missing the beginning of the period, your child misses important directions and information, making it impossible for him or her to keep up with the rest of the class. I hope that we can work together as a team to help make sure that your child attends class. If you have any questions, pleas e stop by before or just after school, or give me a call anytime.

Sincerely,

عزيزي ولي الأمر،

تلميذك يتأخر في الحضور الى الفصل بشكل متكرر بكثرة، وهذا التأخر سوف يضر بأدائه / أدائها. عدم حضور الفترة الاولى من الفصل، سيضيّع عليه توجيهات ومعلومات مهمة، مما سيجعل اللحاق ببقية الطلبة في الفصل عملية مستحيلة. أأمل أن نستطيع العمل معاً كفريق واحد لكي نساعد تلميذك في حضوره للفصل. إذا كانت لديك أية أسئلة فأرجو أن تحضر قبل أو بعد فترة الدراسة، أو الإتصال بي هاتفياً في أي وقت تشاء.

المخلص،

General Resources That School Offers

Dear Parent or Guardian,

The teachers and staff here at school hope to help you and your child in any way we can. The school offers translators and may also be able to help with school supplies and other services. Please feel free to stop by the school office anytime to explore the services available. If you work during the day, you can always call or send a note with your child. We hope to talk to you soon!

Sincerely,

عزيزي ولي الأمر،

يأمل المدرسون والموظفون بالمدرسة أن يقدموا المساعدة لك ولتلميذك بأي طريقة ممكنة . تقدم المدرسة مترجمين ويمكن أن تساعدك أيضاً في التجهيزات الدراسية والخدمات الأخرى. تفضل بالحضور إلى المكتب المختص بالمدرسة في أي وقت للتعرف عن الخدمات المتوفرة. إذا كنت تعمل خلال اليوم، يمكنك دائما أن تتصل بنا هاتفياً أو إرسال مذكرة مع تلميذك. نأمل أن نتكلم معك قريباً. المخلص،

8

Russian

Sem'raz otmer'—odin raz

(Measure seven times before you cut)

CULTURAL FACTS

Russians in the United States

People of Russian descent have a long and complex immigration history in the United States, starting with Russians living in Alaska who became citizens by default when the territory changed hands. Immigration from Russia has generally been in waves, influenced by economic and political stress within Russia (or the former Soviet Union). The first immigrants fled a land shortage in the 1880s, and many took advantage of the Homestead Act in the United States, moving west. With the Bolshevik Revolution of 1917, a new class of Russians immigrated to the United States, namely the members of the ruling and educated class who were divested by the populist redistribution of wealth. This community remained largely urban and was less intent on assimilation than on continuing a traditionally Russian way of life. Continuing through the Cold War era, anti-Russian sentiment within the United States also contributed to the isolation and autonomy of the Russian community. In 1952, embarrassed by the rate at which intellectuals and artists (among them Igor Stravinsky and Vladimir Nabokov) were moving to the United States, the USSR banned emigration. However, with the thaw of the Cold War, the United States is now experiencing a wave of Russian immigration greater than any seen before. Most in this recent wave are young and educated, though not without memory of the turmoil of the twentieth century.

The Russian Language

Russian is the first language of 145 million people, most of whom live in Russia or in the countries of the former USSR. Israel also hosts a large Russian-speaking population, with 750,000 Jewish immigrants from Russia. As would be expected in a language with such a large geographic distribution, there are many Russian dialects, with most linguists grouping these dialects into northern and southern varieties (with Moscow lying in between). Unlike some of the other languages in this book, Russian vocabulary includes almost all modern technical and scientific terms.

Russian Religion and Culture

For many years, religion in Russia was subservient to the state. Russian Orthodox Christianity, which is a distinct branch of the Eastern Orthodox Church and still accounts for about 75 percent of the total religious population, bent its doctrine to justify the actions of the USSR. The number of believers dropped in relation to flagging confidence in government. But with the growth of religious freedom and autonomy in the 1990s, religion has seen resurgence in Russian life, with nearly 40 percent of the population claiming religious affiliation. Islam is the second largest religion among Russians, and communities that follow Buddhism and Judaism exist as well.

In general, Russian culture is well known for arts and education, with a history of state-sponsored theater and free higher education.

Russian Holidays and Other Important Days

January 1-5: The *New Year* is Russia's most popular holiday, sometimes celebrated again on the fourteenth, which is the first day of the Julian calendar, used in Russia until 1918.

January 7: *Russian Orthodox Christmas.*

February 23: *Army Day.*

March 8: *Women's Day.*

May 1: Spring and *Labor Day* are celebrated on or near *Russian Orthodox Easter.*

May 9: *Victory Day* celebrates the end of World War II in Europe.

June 12: *Independence Day* marks the 1991 declaration of Russia's independence from the USSR.

November 4: *Day of National Unity.*

Pronunciation and Alphabet

Russian is spelled phonetically, using the Cyrillic alphabet as shown in the table below.

Cyrillic Alphabet and Phonetic Pronunciation

А	Б	В	Г	Д	Е	Ё	Ж	З	И	Й	К	Л	М	Н
A	B	V	G	D	E	Ё	Zh	Z	I	Ĭ	K	L	M	N
О	П	Р	С	Т	У	Ф	Х	Ц	Ч	Ш	Щ	Э	Ю	Я
O	P	R	S	T	U	F	Kh	Ts	Ch	Sh	Shch	É	Iu	Ia

Communication With Home: Useful Phrases

English	Russian Script	Pronunciation
Parents	Родители	Raditeli
Mother	Мама/Мать	Mama/Mat'
Father	Папа/Отец	Papa/Otyets
Aunt	Тётя	Tyotya
Uncle	Дядя	Dyadya
Brother	Брат	Brat
Sister	Сестра	Sestra
Cousin	Двоюродный брат Двоюродная сестра (Кузен/Кузина)	Dvoyurodnii brat Dvoyurodnaya sestra (Kuzen/Kuzina)
Boyfriend/Girlfriend	Парень/Девушка	Paren'/Devushka
Whom do you live with?	С кем ты живёшь?	S kem ti zhivyosh?
What is your phone number?	Какой у тебя телефон?	Kakoi u tebya telefon?
Please show this note to your ____.	Пожалуйста, покажи эту записку своей (f) / своему (m) ____.	Pazhalusta, pakazhi etu zapisku svayei (f) /svayemu (m) ____.
Please get this signed and bring it back.	Пожалуйста, принеси это обратно с подписью.	Pazhalusta, prinesi eto abratno s podpis'yu.
Please have your ____ call me at school	Пожалуйста, пусть твоя (f) / твой (m) ____ позвонит мне в школу.	Pazhalusta, pust' tvaia (f) / tvoi (m) ____ pazvanit mne v shkolu.

Classroom Communication: Useful Phrases

English	Russian Script	Pronunciation
Sit down please.	Пожалуйста, садитесь. (pl)	Pazhalusta, sadites'. (pl)
The assignment is on the board.	Задание на доске.	Zadaniye na daske.
Pay attention!	Будьте внимательны! (pl)	Bud'te vnimatel'ni! (pl)
Good job.	Молодец.	Molodets.
Excellent!	Замечательно!	Zamechatel'no!
Do you need help?	Тебе помочь?	Tebe pamoch'?
Do you understand?	Ты понимаешь?	Ti panimayesh?
Do you understand the assignment?	Тебе понятно задание?	Tebe panyatno zadaniye?
Thanks for listening.	Спасибо за внимание.	Spasiba za vnimaniye.
Open your book to page ____.	Откройте книгу на странице____.	Atkroite knigu na stranitse ____.
I know it's hard; do the best you can	Я знаю, что это сложно, но постарайся.	Ya znayu, chto eto slozhna; no postaraisya.
How do you say ____ in Russian?	Как будет по-русски ____ ?	Kak budet pa russki ____?
What do you think about ____?	Что ты думаешь о ____?	Chto ti dumayesh' o ____?
I would like you to ____.	Я хочу, чтобы ты ____.	Ya khachu, chtobi ti ____.
Do you know how to ____?	Ты знаешь, как ____?	Ti znayesh' kak ____?
Is this easy or hard?	Это легко или сложно?	Eto lekhko ili slozhna?
Quiet, please.	Пожалуйста, тишина.	Pazhalusta, tishina.
Please be careful.	Пожалуйста, будьте осторожны.	Pazhalusta, bud'te astarozhni.

Student Communication: Useful Phrases

English	Russian Script	Pronunciation
I am new.	Я новенький.	Ya noven'kiy.
I don't speak English.	Я не говорю по-английски.	Ya ne gavaryu pa angliski.
Do you speak ____?	Ты говоришь ____?	Ti gavarish' ____?
I'm from ____.	Я из ____.	Ya iz ____.
I'm sorry.	Извините	Izvinitye.
Excuse me.	Простите	Prastiti.
Thanks.	Спасибо	Spasiba.
My name is ____.	Меня зовут ____.	Menya zavut ____.
Can you help me?	Ты можешь мне помочь?	Ti mozhesh' mne pamoch'?
Where is the ____?	Где находится ____?	Gde nakhoditsya ____?
Can I play?	Можно мне поиграть?	Mozhna mne paigrat'?

Classroom Supplies: Class Dictionary

Book Учебник uchebnik	Computer Компьютер komp'yuter	Crayons Цветной Карандаш tzvetnoi karandash	Eraser Ластик lastik
Folder Папка papka	Glue Клей clay	Markers Фломастеры flamasteri	Note Записка zapiska
Notebook Тетрадь tetrad'	Paint Краска kraska	Paperclip Скрепка skrepka	Pen Ручка ruchka
Pencil Карандаш karandash	Piece of Paper Листок бумаги listok bumagi	Poster Плакат plakat	Printer Принтер printer
Ruler Линейка lineika	Scissors Ножницы nozhnitsi	Stapler Степлер stepler	Tape Лента lenta

School Mechanics: Class Dictionary

Absent	Bathroom	Bell	Cafeteria
Отсутствует atsutstvuyet	Туалеj tualet	Звонок zvanok	Столовая stalovaya
Class Period	Clock	Counselor	To Get a Drink
Урок urok	Часы chasi	Завуч (школьный консультант) zavuch (shkol'nii kan sul'tant)	Пойти попить payti papit'
Gymnasium	Library	Locker	Lunch
Спортзал sportzahl	Библиотека biblioteka	Шкафчик shkafchik	Обед abet
Office	Playground	Principal	Recess
Кабинет kabinet	Игровая площадка igrovaya ploschadka	Директор direktor	Перемена peremena
Schedule	Secretary	Tardy	Teacher
8:30 Welcome/Class Business 9:00 Language Arts 10:30 Mathematics 11:30 Social Studies 12:00 Lunch 1:00 Science 2:00 Art/Music/PE Расписание raspisaniye	Секретарь sekretar'	Опоздавший apazdavshiy	Учительница (f) Учитель (m) uchitel'nitsa (f) uchitel' (m)

Assignment Words: Class Dictionary

Assignment	Correct	Design	Directions
Задание zadaniye	Правильно pravil'no	План/дизайн plan/dizain	Указания ukazaniya
To Discuss	To Draw	Due Date	Grade
Обсуждать' absuzhdat	Рисовать risavat'	Дата сдачи работы data sdachi raboti	Оценка atsenka
To Help	Homework	To Listen	Permission Letter
Помогать pamagat'	Домашнее задание damashneye zadaniye	Слушать slushat'	Записка от родителей (разрешение) zapiska ot raditelei (razresheniye)
Questions	To Read	Stop	To Take Notes
Вопросы vaprosi	Читать chitat'	Остановиться astanavit's'a	Записывать zapisivat'
Test	To Turn In	To Write	Wrong
Тест/Контрольная работа test/kantrol'nayia rabota	Сдавать работу sdavat' rabotu	Писать pisat'	Неправильно nepravil'no

Playground and Physical Education Vocabulary: Class Dictionary

Ball Мяч myach	Baseball Бейсбол beisbol	Basketball Баскетбол basketbol	To Catch Ловить lavit'
To Change Переодеться periadet'sia	Circle Круг krug	Drill Тренироваться treniravat'sia	Field Стадион stadion
To Follow Следовать sledavat'	Football (American) Американский футбол amerikanskiy futbol	Four Square квадратный kvadratnyi	Go in Front Иди впереди idi vperedi
Gym Clothes Спортивная одежда spartivnaia adezhda	Handball гандбол gundball	To Hit бить bit'	Hurt Ушибить ushibit'
To Jump Прыгать prigat'	Jumprope Скакалка skakalka	Kickball Кикбол kickball	Line Очередь ochered'

Lock	Locker Room	To Lose	Out of Bounds
Замок	Раздевалка	Проиграть	Вне игры
zamok	rasdivalka	praigrat'	vne igri
The Rules	To Run	Shoes	Sideline
RULES			
Правила	Бежать/Бегать	Ботинки/Кроссовки	Боковая линия
pravila	bezhat'/begat'	batinki/krasovki	bakavayia liniya
Soccer	Sport	To Stretch	Team
Футбол	Спорт	Потянуться	Команда
futbol	sport	patyanut'sia	kamanda
Tetherball	To Throw	Volleyball	Whistle
Тезербол	Бросать	Волейбол	Свистеть
tezerball	brasat'	volleibol	svistet'

Science Vocabulary: Class Dictionary

Acid	Animal	Base	Climate
Кислота kislata	Животное zhivotnoye	Основание asnavaniye	Климат klimat
Dinosaur	Earth	Electricity	Energy
Динозавр dinazavr	Земля zemlya	Электричество electrichestvo	Энергия energia
Environment	Experiment	Extinct	Hypothesis
Окружающая среда akruzhayushchayia sreda	Опыт/Эксперимент opit/experiment	Вымерший vymershiy	Гипотеза gipoteza
To Investigate	Lab Notebook	Laboratory	Matter
Расследовать rassledovat	Лабораторная тетрадь labaratornaya tetrad'	Лаборатория laboratoriya	Материя materia
Motion	Planet	Plant	Science
Движение dvizhenie	Планета planeta	Растение rasteniye	Наука nauka

Math Vocabulary: Class Dictionary

To Add	Answer	To Calculate	Calculator
+	$1 + 1 = ②$	$\begin{array}{r} 7 \\ 8 \\ +5 \\ \hline 20 \end{array}$	
Складывать skladivat'	Ответ atvet	Считать schitat'	Калькулятор kal'kuliator

To Combine	To Divide	Equation	Exponent
	$\div$	$2 + 3 = 5$	A^4
Объединять ob'yedinyat'	Делить delit'	Уравнение/Формула uravnenie/formula	Показатель степени pakazatel' stepeni

Graph	Math	To Multiply	Numbers
		$3 \otimes 2$	$1\ 2\ 3\ 4\ 5$ $6\ 7\ 8\ 9$
График grafik	Математика matematika	Умножать umnazhat'	Числа chisla

To Order	Problem	Property	To Prove
$1, 2, 3, 4$	$1 + 3 = ?$	$x(y + 2)$	
Располагать в определённом порядке raspalagat' v apredelionom paryadke	Задача zadacha	Показатель pakazatel'	Доказывать dakazyvat'

To Simplify	To Solve	To Subtract	Variable
$\frac{3X + 42}{4} = 6X \longrightarrow X = 2$	$3x=12$ $X=4$	$12 \ominus 6$	x, y
Упрощать upraschat'	Решать reshat'	Вычитать vichitat'	Переменная величина peremennayia velichina

Social Studies Vocabulary: Class Dictionary

Africa	Asia	Australia	Buddhist
Африка	Азия	Австралия	Буддист
afrika	aziya	avstralia	buddist
Christian	Citizenship	Continent	Country
Христианин (m); Христианка (а)	Гражданство	Континент/Материк	Страна
khristianin (m); khristianka (f)	grazhdanstvo	kantinent/materik	strana
Democracy	Europe	Geography	Government
Демократия	Европа	География	Правительство
demokratia	yevropa	giagrafiya	pravitelstvo
Hinduism	History	Jewish	Map
Индуизм	История	Еврейский	Карта
induism	istoriya	yevreiskiy	karta
Muslim	North American	South America	World
Мусульманин (m); Мусульманка (f)	Северная Америка	Южная Америка	Мир
musul'manin (m); musul'manka (f)	severnaya amerika	yuzhnaia amerika	mir

Welcome to My Classroom

Dear Parent or Guardian,

I would like to welcome your child to my classroom. The first couple of weeks can be difficult for students who don't yet speak English, but by working with you as a team I hope to make the transition as smooth as possible. While my Russian is not strong, I will do the best I can to communicate what is expected of your child in the classroom and in the school. Please feel free to stop by before or just after school, or to call anytime.

Again, welcome to our school! I look forward to speaking with you soon.

Sincerely,

Уважаемые родители (опекуны)!

Я очень рад / рада принять Вашего ребёнка в свой класс. Первые несколько недель могут оказаться немного сложными для учеников, пока не говорящих по-английски. Совместными усилиями мы сможем облегчить ребёнку этот переходный период. Я не очень хорошо говорю по-русски, но, тем не менее, я постараюсь объяснить, какие требования предъявляются к Вашему ребёнку в рамках данного класса и школы вообще. Пожалуйста, заходите до или после уроков или звоните в любое время. Ещё раз, добро пожаловать в нашу школу! До скорой встречи.

С уважением,

Your Child Is a Pleasure to Have in Class

Dear Parent or Guardian,

This is a note of thanks to let you know that your child is a pleasure to have in class and to thank you for the work you do at home to help your child succeed. Though your child sometimes has difficulties with the language, he or she is trying hard and making progress every day. Keep up the good work!

Sincerely,

Уважаемые родители (опекуны)!

Этим письмом я хотел бы /хотела бы поблагодарить Вас за то, что Ваш ребёнок учится у меня в классе. Несмотря на то, что он иногда испытывает трудности с языком, я вижу, как он старается, и это даёт положительные результаты. Так держать!

С уважением,

Your Child Is Not Performing Up to Ability

Dear Parent or Guardian,

Though your child is smart and capable, he or she is not performing up to his or her ability. We understand that it's difficult to learn when you don't speak the language, but the only way to learn is to try, and your child needs to try harder. If you have any questions, please stop by before or just after school, or give me a call anytime.

Sincerely,

Уважаемые родители (опекуны)!

Несмотря на способности Вашего ребёнка, он учится хуже своих возможностей. Мы понимаем, что учиться, не зная в достаточной мере языка, сложно. Но без старания ничему не научишься, и Вашему ребёнку надо больше стараться. Если у Вас есть вопросы, пожалуйста, заходите до или после уроков или звоните в любое время.

С уважением,

Please Schedule a Meeting

Dear Parent or Guardian,

Please call or stop by the school office to schedule a meeting concerning your child. We understand that your time is valuable, but this is very important.

Sincerely,

Уважаемые родители (опекуны)!

Просьба позвонить или зайти в школу, чтобы назначить встречу по поводу Вашего ребёнка. Мы понимаем, что Вы очень заняты, но это крайне важно.

С уважением,

I am the parent of _____.

Ай эм дэ пэрэнт оф _____

❑ I need a translator.

❑ Ай нид э трэнслейтэр.

Your Child's Behavior Is a Problem

Dear Parent or Guardian,

Your child's behavior is unacceptable. Not only does your child create an environment where he or she cannot learn, but your child is also disrupting the learning of others. I hope we can work as a team to help your child learn to behave appropriately in school. If your child continues his or her current behavior, it will result in severe disciplinary action. If you have any questions, please stop by before or just after school, or give me a call anytime.

Sincerely,

Уважаемые родители (опекуны)!

Ваш ребёнок ведёт себя недопустимым образом. Он не только создаёт обстановку, в которой невозможно учиться, но и отвлекает от учёбы других. Я надеюсь, что совместными усилиями мы сможем помочь Вашему ребёнку научиться правильно вести себя в школе. Если же Ваш ребёнок и далее будет вести себя подобным образом, нам придётся применить более строгие дисциплинарные меры. Если у Вас есть вопросы, пожалуйста, заходите до или после уроков или звоните в любое время.

С уважением,

Absences Are Hurting Performance

Dear Parent or Guardian,

Your child's absences are hurting his or her performance. Much of what we do in school builds on what we did the day before; if a student is absent it can be very hard to catch up. I hope that we can work together as a team to help make sure that your child attends class. If you have any questions, please stop by before or just after school, or give me a call anytime.

Sincerely,

Уважаемые родители (опекуны)!

Ваш ребёнок пропускает занятия, и это сказывается на его успеваемости. Большинство наших уроков опирается на предыдущий учебный материал. Пропуская занятия, иногда бывает сложно нагнать пропущенный материал. Я надеюсь, что совместными усилиями мы сможем помочь Вашему ребёнку не пропускать уроки. Если у Вас есть вопросы, пожалуйста, заходите до или после уроков или звоните в любое время.

С уважением,

Tardiness Is Hurting Performance

Dear Parent or Guardian,

Your child is frequently late to class, and this tardiness is hurting his or her performance. By missing the beginning of the period, your child misses important directions and information, making it impossible for him or her to keep up with the rest of the class. I hope that we can work together as a team to help make sure that your child attends class. If you have any questions, please stop by before or just after school, or give me a call anytime.

Sincerely,

Уважаемые родители (опекуны)!

Ваш ребёнок часто опаздывает на занятия, и эти опоздания сказываются на его успеваемости. Пропуская начало урока, Ваш ребёнок пропускает указания и важную информацию. что делает невозможным работать вместе со всем классом. Я надеюсь, что совместными усилиями мы сможем помочь Вашему ребёнку не опаздывать на уроки. Если у Вас есть вопросы, пожалуйста, заходите до или после уроков или звоните в любое время.

С уважением,

General Resources That School Offers

Dear Parent or Guardian,

The teachers and staff here at school hope to help you and your child in any way we can. The school offers translators and may also be able to help with school supplies and other services. Please feel free to stop by the school office anytime to explore the services available. If you work during the day, you can always call or send a note with your child. We hope to talk to you soon!

Sincerely,

Уважаемые родители (опекуны)!

Учителя и персонал школы всячески стремятся помочь Вам и Вашему ребёнку. Мы предлагаем услуги переводчиков, а также можем помочь с приобретением школьных принадлежностей и других видов услуг. Пожалуйста, заходите в школу в любое время, чтобы ознакомиться с теми услугами, которые мы предлагаем. Если Вы днем работаете, вы всегда можете позвонить или передать записку со своим ребёнком. До скорой встречи!

С уважением,

9

Tagalog

Ang hindi marunong lumingon sa pinanggalingan,
ay hindi makakarating sa paroroonan

(He who doesn't know his past will not know where he is going)

CULTURAL FACTS

Tagalog in the United States

As a result of the Spanish-American War, the Philippines became a U.S. protectorate, and between 1898 and 1946, Filipinos entered the United States as nationals (though not without discrimination). During this time, many immigrated to California and Hawaii as farm workers, or to the Pacific Northwest for jobs in the timber and fishing industries. These immigrants called themselves *Pinoy*, which came to denote a person of Filipino descent who lived in a foreign land but retained Filipino culture and language. When the Philippines gained their independence in 1946, immigration slowed until 1965, when the Immigration Act drew many Filipino professionals to the United States. The U.S. Navy also continued to recruit Filipinos, who, after serving, gained U.S. citizenship. Later immigrants increasingly sought refuge from political, economic, and social turmoil (notably under Ferdinand Marcos, who was president of the Philippines from 1965 to 1986). Recently, the Philippine government has been under threat from armed communist insurgents and from Muslim separatists, conditions that have led to increased immigration to the United States from the Philippines.

The Tagalog Language

Filipino, the official language of the Philippines, is based on Tagalog, the first language of most Filipino ELL students in the United States. Tagalog is an Austronesian language, related to languages spoken in Hawaii, Samoa, and Indonesia. Speakers of Tagalog from all societal levels commonly incorporate non-Tagalog words into their speech in a technique known as *code switching*. The hybrid that combines Tagalog and English is known as *Taglish*. The Tagalog language also includes a kind of slang known as *binaliktád*, or "backward speech" in which syllables may be reversed (making the word *pater*, which means father, into *erpat*). When speaking in Tagalog to an elder, every sentence should end with *po* or *ho*, which shows respect.

Filipino Religion and Culture

The Philippines was a Spanish colony from 1521 to 1898 and retains many Spanish traditions, including surnames and influences on food, architecture, religion, and literature. Today, about 80 percent of Filipinos are Roman Catholic, with thriving Protestant and Muslim minorities.

Many Filipinos also believe in the anting-anting or amulet. These amulets, which represent belief in a synthesis of Catholicism and animism, are sold together with herbs prescribed by local healers outside Catholic churches such as Quiapo Church in the heart of downtown Manila.

The distribution of the population over more than seven thousand distinct islands of the Philippines leads to a multicultural society, with about 120 different ethnic groups. Many classify these ethnicities under the three headings of sea-going, lowland, and mountainous peoples.

Filipino Holidays and Other Important Days

In addition to the holidays of the Catholic year, Filipinos celebrate these holidays:

January 1: *Bagong Taon* (New Year)

January 6: *Araw ng Tatlong Hari* (Three Kings' Day)

February 14: *Araw ng mga Puso* (Valentine's Day)

June 12: *Araw ng Kalayaan* (Independence Day)

July 4: *Filipino-American Friendship Day*

November 1: *Undas ng mga Patay* (All Saints' Day)

November 2: *Araw ng mga Kaluluwa* (All Souls' Day)

December 16-24: *Misa de Gallo* (Early Morning Mass)

December 30: *Awar ng mga Bayani* (National Heroes' Day)

Pronunciation and Alphabet

The Tagalog alphabet originally included twenty letters, was then expanded to thirty-three, and now includes twenty-eight letters, adding ñ and *ng* to the Latin alphabet. The letter ñ sounds like the *ni* in onion, and the letter *ng*, called the nasal velar, sounds like *nk* in "bank." While Tagalog is not technically a tonal language, differences in stressed syllables can alter word meaning. And while not by any means a Romance language, the commonly used Latin alphabet as pronounced naturally by English speakers succeeds in approximating Tagalog better than it does many other languages that have adopted the Latin alphabet.

Communication With Home: Useful Phrases

English	Tagalog	Pronunciation Guide
Parents	Manga magulang	Ma-nga ma-gu-lang
Mother	Ina	I-na
Father	Ama	A-ma
Aunt	Tiya	Ti-ya
Uncle	Tiyo	Ti-yo
Brother	Kapatid na lalaki	Ka-pa-tid na la-la-ki
Sister	Kapatid na babae	Ka-pa-tid na ba-ba-e
Cousin	Pinsan	Pin-san
Boyfriend/Girlfriend	Kasintahang Lalaki/Kasintahang Babae	Ka-sin-ta-hang la-la-ki/ka-sin-ta-hang ba-ba-e
Whom do you live with?	Sino ang kasama mo sa bahay?	Si-no ang ka-sa-ma mo sa ba-hay?
What is your phone number?	Ano ang iyong numero ng telepono?	A-no ang i-yong nu-mero ng te-le-pono?
Please show this note to your ____.	Mangyaring ipakita ang maikling liham na ito sa iyong ____.	Mang-ya-ring i-pa-kita ang ma-ik-ling li-ham na i-to sa i-yong ____.
Please get this signed and bring it back.	Mangyaring papirmahan ito at ibalik.	Mang-ya-ring pa-pirma-han i-to at i-ba-lik.
Please have your ____ call me at school.	Mangyaring sabihin sa iyong ____ na tawagan ako sa paaralan.	Mang-ya-ring sa-bi-hin sa i-yong ____ na ta-wa-gan a-ko sa paaralan.

Classroom Communication: Useful Phrases

English	Tagalog	Pronunciation Guide
Sit down please.	Maupo lamang.	Ma-u-po la-mang.
The assignment is on the board.	Ang takdang-aralin ay nasa pisara.	Ang tak-dang a-ra-lin ay na-sa pi-sa-ra.
Pay attention!	Makinig!	Ma-ki-nig!
Good job.	Magaling na trabaho.	Ma-ga-ling na tra-ba-ho.
Excellent!	Mahusay!	Ma-hu-say!
Do you need help?	Kailangan mo ba ng tulong?	Ka-i-la-ngan mo ba ng tu-long?
Do you understand ____?	Naiintindihan mo ba na ____?	Na-i-in-tin-di-han mo ba na ____?
Do you understand the assignment?	Naiintindihan mo ba ang takdang-aralin?	Na-i-in-tin-dihan mo ba ang tak-dang a-ra-lin?
Thanks for listening.	Salamat sa pakikinig.	Sa-la-mat sa pa-ki-ki-nig.
Open your book to page ____.	Buksan ang iyong libro sa pahina ____.	Buk-san ang i-yong lib-ro sa pahina____.
I know it's hard; do the best you can.	Alam kong mahirap ito; gawin ang magagawa mo.	A-lam kong ma-hi-rap ito; ga-win ang ma-ga-ga-wa mo.
How do you say ____ in Tagalog?	Paano mo sasabihin ang ____ sa Tagalog?	Pa-a-no mo sa-sa-bi-hin ang ____ sa Ta-ga-log?
What do you think about ____?	Ano ang palagay mo sa ____?	A-no ang pa-la-gay mo sa ____?
I would like you to ____.	Gusto ko na ikaw ay ____.	Gus-to ko na i-kaw ay ____.
Do you know how to ____?	Alam mo ba kung paano ____?	A-lam mo ba kung pa-a-no ____?
Is this easy or hard?	Ito ba ay madali o mahirap?	Ito ba ay ma-da-li o ma-hi-rap?
Quiet, please.	Mangyaring tumahimik.	Mang-ya-ring tu-ma-hi-mik.
Please be careful.	Mag-ingat.	Mag-i-ngat.

Student Communication: Useful Phrases

English	Tagalog	Pronunciation Guide
I am new.	Ako ay bago.	A-ko ay ba-go.
I don't speak English.	Hindi ako nagsasalita ng Ingles.	Hin-di a-ko nag-sa-sa-li-ta ng ing-les.
Do you speak ____?	Nagsasalita ka ba ng ____?	Nag-sa-sa-li-ta ka ba ng ____?
I'm from ____.	Ako ay mula sa ____.	A-ko ay mu-la sa ____.
I'm sorry.	Humihingi ako ng paumanhin/ Sorry.	Hu-mi-hi-ngi ako ng pa-u-man-hin/so-rry.
Excuse me.	Pasensiya na.	Pa-sen-si-ya na.
Thanks.	Salamat.	Sa-la-mat.
My name is ____.	Ang pangalan ko ay ____.	Ang pa-nga-lan ko ay ____.
Can you help me?	Puwede mo ba akong tulungan?	Pu-we-de mo ba a-kong tu-lu-ngan?
Where is the ____?	Nasaan ang ____?	Na-sa-an ang ____?
Can I play?	Puwede ba akong maglaro?	Pu-we-de ba a-kong mag-laro?

Classroom Supplies: Class Dictionary

Book Libro li-bro	Computer Kompyuter kom-pyuter	Crayons Krayola kra-yo-la	Eraser Pambura pam-bura
Folder Polder pol-der	Glue Pandikit pan-dee-keet	Markers Manga pangmarka ma-nga pang-marka	Note Maikling sulat ma-ik-ling su-lat
Notebook Kuwaderno ku-wa-derno	Paint Pintura pin-tu-ra	Paperclip Klip ng papel klip ng Pa-pel	Pen Pluma plu-ma
Pencil Lapis la-pis	Piece of Paper Piraso ng papel pi-ra-so ng pa-pel	Poster Paskil pas-kil	Printer Printer print-er
Ruler Ruler ru-ler	Scissors Gunting gun-ting	Stapler Pang-isteypol pang-is-tey-pol	Tape Pandikit pan-dee-keet

School Mechanics: Class Dictionary

Absent	Bathroom	Bell	Cafeteria
Lumiban/Absent lu-mi-ban/ab-sent	Banyo ban-yo	Kampana kam-pa-na	Kapiterya ka-pi-terya
Class Period	Clock	Counselor	To Get a Drink
Oras ng klase o-ras ng kla-se	Orasan o-ra-san	Tagapayo ta-ga-pa-yo	Uminom u-mi-nom
Gymnasium	Library	Locker	Lunch
Himnasyo/Gym him-nas-yo/gym	Aklatan ak-la-tan	Laker la-ker	Tanghalian tang-ha-li-an
Office	Playground	Principal	Recess
Tanggapan tang-ga-pan	Palaruan pa-la-ru-an	Punong-guro pu-nong-gu-ro	Pamamahinga/recess pa-ma-ma-hi-nga/re-cess
Schedule	Secretary	Tardy	Teacher
Talaorasan/iskedyul ta-la-o-ra-san/i-sked-yul	Kalihim ka-li-him	Huli hu-li	Guro gu-ro

Assignment Words: Class Dictionary

Assignment	Correct	Design	Directions
Takdang-aralin	Tama	Disenyo	Manga tagubilin
tak-dang-a-ra-lin	ta-ma	di-sen-yo	ma-nga ta-gu-bi-lin
To Discuss	**To Draw**	**Due Date**	**Grade**
Talakayin	Gumuhit	Petsa kung kailan dapat matanggap	Marka
ta-la-ka-yin	gu-mu-hit	pet-sa kung ka-i-lan da-pat ma-tang-gap	mar-ka
To Help	**Homework**	**To Listen**	**Permission Letter**
Tumulong	Gawaing-bahay	Makinig	Liham ng pahintulot
tu-mu-long	ga-wa-ing-ba-hay	ma-ki-nig	li-ham ng pa-hin-tulot
Questions	**To Read**	**Stop**	**To Take Notes**
Manga katanungan	Magbasa	Tumigil	Magtala
ma-nga ka-ta-nu-ngan	mag-ba-sa	tu-mi-gil	mag-ta-la
Test	**To Turn In**	**To Write**	**Wrong**
Pagsusulit	Ibigay	Magsulat	Mali
pag-su-su-lit	i-bi-gay	mag-su-lat	ma-li

Playground and Physical Education Vocabulary: Class Dictionary

Ball	Baseball	Basketball	To Catch
Bola	Beysbol	Basketbol	Sambutin/Saluhin
bo-la	beys-bol	bas-ket-bol	sam-butin/sa-lu-hin

To Change	Circle	Drill	Field
Magpalit	Bilog	Magpraktis	Palaruan
mag-palit	bi-log	mag-prak-tis	pa-la-ruan

To Follow	Football (American)	Four Square	Go in Front
Sundin	Putbol	Apat na kwadrado	Punta sa harapan
sun-din	put-bol	a-pat na kwad-ra-do	poon-tah sa ha-ra-pan

Gym Clothes	Handball	To Hit	Hurt
Manga damit na panghimnasyo/pang-gym		Hit	Nasaktan
ma-nga da-mit na pang-him-nasyo/pang-gym	Hagisang bola	hit	na-sak-tan
	ha-ghee-sang bo-la		

To Jump	Jumprope	Kickball	Line
Lumundag	Luksong lubid	Sipangbola	Linya
lu-mun-dag	look-song loo-bid	see-pang bo-la	lin-ya

Lock	Locker Room	To Lose	Out of Bounds
Kandado	Laker na silid	Matalo	Labas ng hangganan
kan-da-do	la-ker na si-lid	ma-ta-lo	la-bas ng hang-ga-nan
The Rules	To Run	Shoes	Sideline
Ang Manga tuntunin	Tumakbo	Sapatos	Hangganang guhit/sideline
ang ma-nga tun-tu-nin	tu-mak-bo	sa-pa-tos	hang-ga-nang gu-hit/side-line
Soccer	Sport	To Stretch	Team
Saker	Palakasan	mag-unat	Koponan/Pangkat
sa-ker	pa-la-ka-san	mag-u-nat	ko-po-nan/pang-kat
Tetherball	To Throw	Volleyball	Whistle
Balikang bola	Ihagis	Balibol	Sumilbato
ba-lee-kang bo-la	i-ha-gis	ba-li-bol	su-mil-bato

Science Vocabulary: Class Dictionary

Acid	Animal	Base	Climate
Asido	Hayop	Beys	Klima
a-si-do	ha-yop	beys	kli-ma
Dinosaur	Earth	Electricity	Energy
Dinosauro	Mundo	Kuryente	Enerhiya
di-no-sa-u-ro	moon-do	kur-yen-te	ener-hi-ya
Environment	Experiment	Extinct	Hypothesis
Kapaligiran	Eksperimento	Patay na	Haka
ka-pa-li-gi-ran	eks-pe-ri-men-to	pa-ta-y na	ha-ka
To Investigate	Lab Notebook	Laboratory	Matter
Mag-imbestiga	Kuwaderno sa laboratoryo	Laboratoryo	Bagay
mag eem-bess-tee-gha	ku-wa-derno sa la-bo-ra-tor-yo	la-bo-ra-to-ryo	ba-ghai
Motion	Planet	Plant	Science
Galaw	Planeta	Halaman	Agham
gha-lau	pla-ne-ta	ha-la-man	ag-ham

Math Vocabulary: Class Dictionary

To Add **+** Magdagdag mag-dag-dag	Answer 1 + 1 = ② Sagot sa-got	To Calculate 7 8 +5 20 Magkalkula mag-kal-kula	Calculator Makinang pangkuwenta/ Calculator Ma-ki-nang pang-ku-we- nta/Cal-cu-la-tor
To Combine Pagsamahin pag-sa-ma-hin	To Divide ÷ Maghati mag-hati	Equation 2 + 3 = 5 Pagpapareho pag-pa-pa-re-ho	Exponent A^4 Exponent ex-po-nent
Graph Grap grap	Math Matematika ma-te-ma-tika	To Multiply 3 ⊗ 2 Imultiplika i-mul-tip-li-ka	Numbers 1 2 3 4 5 6 7 8 9 Manga numero ma-nga nu-me-ro
To Order 1, 2, 3, 4 Mag-ayos mag-a-yos	Problem 1 + 3 = ? Tanong ta-nong	Property x(y + 2) Katangian ka-ta-ngi-an	To Prove Patunayan pa-tu-na-yan
To Simplify $\frac{3X + 42}{4} = 6X \longrightarrow X = 2$ Gawing simple ga-wing sim-ple	To Solve 3x=12 X=4 Lutasin lu-ta-sin	To Subtract 12 ⊖ 6 Magbawas mag-ba-was	Variable x, y Napagbabagu-bago na-pag-ba-ba-gu-ba-go

Social Studies Vocabulary: Class Dictionary

Africa Aprika ap-ri-ka	Asia Asya as-ya	Australia Australya aws-tral-ya	Buddhist Buddhist boo-diz
Christian Kristiyano kris-ti-ya-no	Citizenship Nasyonalidad nas-yo-na-lee-dad	Continent Kontinente kon-ti-nen-te	Country Bansa ban-sa
Democracy Demokrasya de-mok-ras-ya	Europe Europa eu-ro-pa	Geography Heograpiya he-o-gra-pi-ya	Government gobyerno gob-yer-no
Hinduism Hinduismo hin-doo-ees-mo	History Kasaysayan ka-say-sa-yan	Jewish Hudyo hud-yo	Map Mapa ma-pa
Muslim Muslim mus-lim	North American Hilagang Amerika hi-la-gang a-me-ri-ka	South America Timog Amerika ti-mog a-me-ri-ka	World Daigdig da-ig-dig

Welcome to My Classroom

Dear Parent or Guardian,

I would like to welcome your child to my classroom. The first couple of weeks can be difficult for students who don't yet speak English, but by working with you as a team I hope to make the transition as smooth as possible. While my Tagalog is not strong, I will do the best I can to communicate what is expected of your child in the classroom and in the school. Please feel free to stop by before or just after school, or to call anytime.

Again, welcome to our school! I look forward to speaking with you soon.

Sincerely,

Mahal Naming Magulang o Tagapangalaga,

Malugod kong tinatanggap ang inyong anak sa aking silid-aralan. Ang mga unang linggo ay maaaring maging mahirap para sa mga estudyante na hindi pa nagsasalita ng Ingles, pero sa pamamagitan ng ating pagtutulungan bilang isang pangkat, umaasa ako na magagawang madali ang pagbabago ng kalagayan. Kahit ang Tagalog ko ay hindi mahusay, gagawin ko ang aking magagawa upang masabi kung ano ang inaasahan sa inyong anak sa silid-aralan at sa paaralan. Mangyaring huwag mag-atubiling bumisita bago o pagkatapos na pagkatapos ng klase, o tumawag anumang oras.

Nais ko muling sabihin na malugod namin kayong tinatanggap sa ating paaralan! Umaasa ako na makakausap kayo sa madaling panahon.

Matapat na sumasainyo,

Your Child Is a Pleasure to Have in Class

Dear Parent or Guardian,

This is a note of thanks to let you know that your child is a pleasure to have in class and to thank you for the work you do at home to help your child succeed. Though your child sometimes has difficulties with the language, he or she is trying hard and making progress every day. Keep up the good work!

Sincerely,

Mahal Naming Magulang o Tagapangalaga,

Ito ay isang maikling liham ng pasasalamat upang ipagbigay-alam sa inyo na ikinalulugod namin na makasama ang inyong anak sa klase. Bagaman ang inyong estudyante ay nahihirapan kung minsan sa wika, nagsisikap siya at umuunlad sa bawat araw. Ipagpatuloy po ninyo ang mahusay na gawain!

Matapat na sumasainyo,

Your Child Is Not Performing Up to Ability

Dear Parent or Guardian,

Though your child is smart and capable, he or she is not performing up to his or her ability. We understand that it's difficult to learn when you don't speak the language, but the only way to learn is to try, and your child needs to try harder. If you have any questions, please stop by before or just after school, or give me a call anytime.

Sincerely,

Mahal Naming Magulang o Tagapangalaga,

Bagaman ang inyong estudyante ay matalino at may-kakaya-han, hindi siya nakakaganap ng hanggang sa abot ng kanyang katalinuhan. Naiintindihan namin na mahirap matuto kapag hindi kayo nagsasalita ng wika, pero ang tanging paraan upang matuto ay ang magsikap at kailangan ng inyong estudyante na higit na magsikap. Kung mayroon kayong mga katanungan, mangyaring bumisita bago o pagkatapos na pagkatapos ng klase, o tawagan ako anumang oras.

Matapat na sumasainyo,

Please Schedule a Meeting

Dear Parent or Guardian,

Please call or stop by the school office to schedule a meeting concerning your child. We understand that your time is valuable, but this is very important.

Sincerely,

Mahal Naming Magulang o Tagapangalaga,

Mangyaring tumawag o bumisita sa tanggapan ng paaralan upang itakda ang pulong tungkol sa inyong estudyante. Naiintindihan namin na mahalaga ang inyong oras, pero ito po ay napakahalaga.

Matapat na sumasainyo,

I am the parent of _____.

Ako ang magulang ni _____.

❏ I need a translator.

❏ Kailangan ko ng tagapagsalin-wika.

Your Child's Behavior Is a Problem

Dear Parent or Guardian,

Your child's behavior is unacceptable. Not only does your child create an environment where he or she cannot learn, but your child is also disrupting the learning of others. I hope we can work as a team to help your child learn to behave appropriately in school. If your child continues his or her current behavior, it will result in severe disciplinary action. If you have any questions, please stop by before or just after school, or give me a call anytime.

Sincerely,

Mahal Naming Magulang o Tagapangalaga,

Ang kilos ng inyong estudyante ay hindi katanggap-tanggap. Siya ay hindi lamang gumagawa ng kapaligiran kung saan hindi siya matututo, kundi nagagambala rin niya ang pag-aaral ng iba. Umaasa ako na maaari tayong magtulungan bilang isang pangkat upang tulungan ang inyong estudyante na matutong kumilos nang angkop sa paaralan. Kung ipagpapatuloy ng inyong estudyante ang kanyang kasalukuyang mga kilos, ito ay magbubunga ng mahigpit na aksyong pandisiplina. Kung mayroon kayong mga katanungan, mangyaring bumisita bago o pagkatapos na pagkatapos ng klase, o tawagan ako anumang oras.

Matapat na sumasainyo,

Absences Are Hurting Performance

Dear Parent or Guardian,

Your child's absences are hurting his or her performance. Much of what we do in school builds on what we did the day before; if a student is absent it can be very hard to catch up. I hope that we can work together as a team to help make sure that your child attends class. If you have any questions, please stop by before or just after school, or give me a call anytime.

Sincerely,

Mahal Naming Magulang o Tagapangalaga,

Ang mga hindi pagpasok ng inyong estudyante sa paaralan ay nakakapinsala sa kanyang pagganap. Karamihan ng mga ginagawa sa paaralan ay pagsulong ng ginawa namin sa nakaraang araw; kung ang estudyante ay absent, maaaring maging napakahirap para sa kanya na makahabol. Umaasa ako na makakapagtulungan tayo bilang isang pangkat upang makatulong na masiguro na ang inyong estudyante ay dumadalo sa klase. Kung mayroon kayong mga katanungan, mangyaring bumisita bago o pagkatapos na pagkatapos ng klase, o tawagan ako anumang oras.

Matapat na sumasainyo,

Tardiness Is Hurting Performance

Dear Parent or Guardian,

Your child is frequently late to class, and this tardiness is hurting his or her performance. By missing the beginning of the period, your child misses important directions and information, making it impossible for him or her to keep up with the rest of the class. I hope that we can work together as a team to help make sure that your child attends class. If you have any questions, please stop by before or just after school, or give me a call anytime.

Sincerely,

Mahal Naming Magulang o Tagapangalaga,

Ang inyong estudyante ay madalas na huli sa klase, at ito ay nakakapinsala sa kanyang pagganap. Kapag hindi nakadalo sa simula ng oras ng klase, hindi nakukuha ng inyong anak ang mga mahahalagang tagubilin at impormasyon, at ginagawa nitong imposible para sa kanya na makaagapay sa mga kamag-aral. Umaasa ako na makakapagtulungan tayo bilang isang pangkat upang makatulong na masiguro na ang inyong anak ay dumadalo sa klase. Kung mayroon kayong mga katanungan, mangyaring bumisita bago o pagkatapos na pagkatapos ng klase, o tawagan ako anumang oras.

Matapat na sumasainyo,

General Resources That School Offers

Dear Parent or Guardian,

The teachers and staff here at school hope to help you and your child in any way we can. The school offers translators and may also be able to help with school supplies and other services. Please feel free to stop by the school office anytime to explore the services available. If you work during the day, you can always call or send a note with your child. We hope to talk to you soon!

Sincerely,

Mahal Naming Magulang o Tagapangalaga,

Ang mga guro at mga tauhan ng paaralan ay umaasa na matutulungan kayo at ang inyong estudyante sa anumang paraan na magagawa namin. Ang paaralan ay nag-aalay ng mga tagapagsalin-wika at maaari ring makatulong sa mga gamit sa paaralan at ibang mga serbisyo. Mangyaring huwag mag-atubiling bumisita sa tanggapan ng paaralan anumang oras upang mapag-aralan ang mga serbisyong makukuha. Kung nagtatrabaho kayo sa araw, lagi kayong makakatawag o maka-kapagpadala ng maikling liham sa inyong estudyante. Umaasa kami na makakausap namin kayo sa madaling panahon!

Matapat na sumasainyo,

10

Navajo

T'áá hó ájit'éego éiyá

(*It is up to the individual to achieve*)

CULTURAL FACTS

Navajo in the United States

The 27,000 square miles of the Navajo Nation, encompassing parts of Arizona, New Mexico, and Utah, make it bigger than ten states in the United States. Today more than 300,000 people claim Navajo ancestry. Some dislike the name *Navajo*, which means "takers of the fields," and many prefer to be known by the traditional name Diné, which means "the people." Also living within the boundaries of the Navajo Nation are groups of Apache, who share common roots with the Navajo, and Hopi, who have historically been involved in land disputes with the Navajo. Though livestock and art (especially weaving and jewelry making) have been the mainstays of the Navajo economy, recently the Navajo Nation has negotiated deals with New Mexico and Arizona that allow the development of casinos on Navajo land. In 2002, the average per-capita income in the Navajo Nation was $15,917, or 52 percent of the national average.

The Navajo Language

Also known as *Diné bizaad*, Navajo is an Athabaskan language related to those of Northwest Canada and Alaska. It is similar to the Apache language but completely unrelated to other native Southwest languages. In mainstream U.S. culture, the most famous use of Diné bizaad was during World War II, when Navajo "code talkers" transmitted radio messages on the battlefield. This shows the difficulty that most nonnative speakers have with the language. In general, Navajo is a verb-heavy language, adding a few nouns and using no adjectives.

Navajo Religion and Culture

We the five-fingered beings are related to the four-legged, the winged beings, the spiritual beings, Father Sky, Mother Earth, and nature. We are all relatives. We cannot leave our relatives behind.

—Betty Tso, traditional Navajo

This quote illustrates the Navajo connection to the land, specifically to the land of the Navajo Nation between the four mountains of Blanca Peak in Colorado, Mount Taylor in New Mexico, the San Francisco Peaks in Arizona, and Hesperus Peak in Colorado. According to tradition, the Creator placed the Navajo people on this land and instructed them never to leave. Pauline Whitesinger, a Big Mountain elder, said of this sacred land, "In our traditional tongue, there is no word for relocation. To relocate is to move away and disappear."

Today, Navajo culture is seeing resurgence, as younger generations show increased interest in and respect for old ways. For example, at Diné College at Tsaile, AZ, students learn through the Navajo system of *Sa'ah Naagháí Bik'eh Hózhóón*, applying *Nitsáhákees* (Thinking), *Nahatá* (Planning), *Iiná* (Living), and *Sihasin* (Assurance).

Navajo Holidays and Other Important Days

January 25–February 2: Festival honoring the coming agricultural season. Traditionally, during this time Spider Woman helped the twin brothers Naymezyani and Tobadzistsini defeat the powers of evil.

February 23–March 3: Blessing of the fields and ceremonies for Changing Woman, who has the power to change the world.

September 17–September 25: Harvest festival.

In addition to yearly festivals, the Navajo perform many ceremonies, for blessings, rites, and observances.

Pronunciation and Alphabet

There are three tones in the Navajo language: high, rising, and falling. Using the vowel *e* as an example, the high tone is marked *é*, the rising tone is marked *e'* and the falling tone is marked *è*. In addition to these tones, the Navajo language uses a number of sounds foreign to the English language, including rearticulated vowels (such as *aa* or *aoo*). More detailed discussion of the non-English sounds of the Navajo language can be found online or in one of the following published resources:

- *Diné bizaad: Speak, read, write Navajo.* Irvy Goosen. Flagstaff, AZ: Salina Bookshelf, 1995.
- Talk now! Learn Navajo [CD-ROM]. Renton, WA: Topics Entertainment, 2004.
- *Breakthrough Navajo: An introductory course.* Alan Wilson. Madison, CT: Audio Forum, 1992.

Communication With Home: Useful Phrases

English	Navajo	Pronunciation Guide
Parents	**Amá dóó azhé'é**	A-ma do a-sh-e-e
Mother	**Amá**	A-ma
Father	**Azhé'é**	A-sh-e-e
Aunt	**Amá yázhí**	A-ma ya-sh-ee
Uncle	**Ayáázh / adá'í**	A-ya-sh/A-da-ee
Little brother	**Atsilí**	A-si-l-ee
Little sister	**Adeezhí**	A-day-sh-ee
Cousin	**Azeedí**	A-zay-d-ee
Boyfriend/Girlfriend	**Hwe'ashkii / hwe'at'ééd**	Whe-ash-kee/Whe-a-tayd
Whom do you live with?	**Háísh bił nighan?**	Hay-sh bil ni-gon?
What is your phone number?	**Ha'iísh nifóon namboo?**	Ha-ee-sh ni-fon nam-bo?
Please show this note to your ____.	**Díí naaltsoos ni ____ baa dííłtsos.**	Dee naa-l-sos ni ____ ba dee-l-sos.
Please get this signed and bring it back.	**Díí ná sáan ádoolnííł dóó nídííłtsos.**	Dee na san a-do-l-neel do ni-deel-sos.
Please have your ____ call me at school.	**Ni ____ shich'į' hodoolnih ólta'di.**	Ni ____ shi-chi ho-do-l-ni o-l-ta-di.

Classroom Communication: Useful Phrases

English	Navajo	Pronunciation Guide
Sit down please.	Ńdaah táá shǫǫdi.	N-da taa-sho-di.
The assignment is on the board.	Ádadoołííłígíí bikáá' ak'e'elchíhí bikáá'.	A-da-do-l-nee-lee-gee bi-ka a-ke-el-chi-hi bi-ka.
Pay attention!	Da'íísínółts'ą́ą́'	Da-ee-si-no-l-sa!
Good job.	Nizhónígo į̨nílaa.	Ni-sho-ni-go eeni-laa.
Excellent!	Nizhóní	Ni-shi-ni!
Do you need help?	Níká iishyeedísh?	Ni-ka eesh-y-ay-dish?
Do you understand?	Bik'i'dinitį̨hísh?	Bi-ki-dee-tee-hish?
Do you understand the assignment?	Ádíílíłígíísh bik'i'dinitį̨h?	A-dee-lee-l-I-geesh bi-ki-dee-tee?
Thanks for listening.	Ahéhee' íísínółts'ą́ą́'go.	A-he-he ee-si-nil-sa-go.
Open your book to page ____.	Ninaaltsoos ____ gone'é aa'ánílééh.	Ni-na-l-sos ____ go-ne a-a- ni-lay.
I know it's hard; do the best you can.	Eiłą́ą́ nanitł'ah; t'áá bíninil'ą́ą́nigo ánílééh.	Ay-la na-ni-la; ta bi-ni-ni-l-a-go a-ni-lay.
How do you say ____ in Navajo?	Haash yit'áo ____ ájiniih diné k'ehjí?	Hash yi-tay-go ____ ji-nee di-ne ke-ji?
What do you think about ____?	Hait'áo ____ baa nitsíníkees?	Hay-ta-go ____ ba ni-sin-I-kay-s?
I would like you to ____.	____ kódíínííł.	____ ko-dee-neel.
Do you know how to ____?	____ ísh bééhonísin?	____ ish bay-ho-ni-sin?
Is this easy or hard?	Díísh doo nanitł'ah da éí doodago nanitł'ahish?	Deesh do na-ni-la da ay do-da-go na-ni-la-ish?
Quiet, please.	Ge' táá shǫǫdi.	Ge taa-sho-di.
Please be careful.	Hazhó'ó.	Ha-sho-o.

Student Communication: Useful Phrases

English	Navajo	Pronunciation Guide
I am new.	**Índídah atah niya.**	Ee-ni-da a-ta-nee-ya.
I don't speak English.	**Bilagáana k'ehjí doo yáshti' da.**	Bi-la-ga-na ke-ji do yash-ti da.
Do you speak ____?	**____ jíísh yáníłti'?**	____ Jeesh ya-nil-ti?
I'm from ____.	**____ déé' naashá.**	____ Day na-sha.
I'm sorry.	**Áadoo ándeeshłį́įłgóó ásdzaa.**	A-do a-n-day-shi-eel-goo as-zaa
Excuse me.	**Shá hooł`aah.**	Sha ho-la.
Thanks.	**Ahéhee'.**	A-he-he.
My name is ____.	**____ yinishyé.**	____ yi-nish-ye.
Can you help me?	**Shíká anilyeed ya'?**	Shi-ka a-deel-wol?
Where is the ____?	**Háádish ____?**	Ha-dish ____?
Can I play?	**Naashné ya?**	Na-sh-ne ya?

Classroom Supplies: Class Dictionary

Book	Computer	Crayons	Eraser
Naaltsoos wólta'ígíí	**Béésh bee hane'e t'áá bí nitsékeesígíí**	**Bee na'ach'ąąhí**	**Bee kee alchx—hí**
na-l-sos wo-l-ta-i-gee	bay-sh bay ha-ne-e ta bi ni-se-kay-s	bay-na-a-cha-he	bee-kee-aal-choo-hi
Folder	Glue	Markers	Note
Naaltsoos biih ná'nilí	**bee'idiil'jeehi**	**Bee na'ach'ąąhí**	**Naaltsoos**
na-l-sos bee na-ni-li	be-e-dil-ja-he	bay na-a-chaa-hi	na-l-tsos
Notebook	Paint	Paperclip	Pen
Naaltsoos	**Bee adleeshí**	**Naaltsoos bił dah nátíhí**	**Bee ak'e'elchíhí**
na-l-sos	bay a-d-l-ay-shi	na-l-sos bil da na-ti-hi	bay a-ke-el-chi-hi
Pencil	Piece of Paper	Poster	Printer
Bee ak'e'elchíhí	**Naaltsoos**	**Naaltsoos**	**Béésh ak'e'elchíhí**
bay a-ke-el-chi-hi	na-l-sos	na-l-sos	bay-sh a-ke-el-chi-hi
Ruler	Scissors	Stapler	Tape
Bee í'neel'aahí	**Béésh ahédilí**	**Bee ałhída'iilcha'í**	**idadiil'jeehi**
bay i-nel-a-hi	bay a-he-dil-i	bay a-hi-da-il-cha-hi	eda-del-ja-he

School Mechanics: Class Dictionary

Absent	Bathroom	Bell	Cafeteria
Doo kǫǫ sidáa da	**Tá'ádazdigis góne'é**	**Yoo'**	**Da'adání góne'é**
do-ko-si-da-da	ta-a-daz-di-gis go-ne-e	yooh	da-a-da-ni go-ne-e

Class Period	Clock	Counselor	To Get a Drink
Na'nitin góne'	**Ná'oolkiłí**	**Achį'yáłti'ii**	**Ajidlą**
na-ni-tin go-ne	na-ol-ki-li	a-chi-yaal-ti-ee	a-ji-la

Gymnasium	Library	Locker	Lunch
Jooł bee na'a'nehí góne'	**Naaltsoos sinil góne'é**	**T'áadoo le'é bįįh ná'niłí**	**Ałníní'áago da'adą**
jol bay na-a-ne-hi go-ne	na-l-sos si-nil go-ne-e	ta-do le-e bee na-ni-li	al-ni-ni-a-go da-a-da

Office	Playground	Principal	Recess
Bídahólnįhí nidaalnish góne'é	**Daa'nee'bahaz'anigi**	**Olta' binaatáanii**	**Ch'ééjíjahgo**
bi-da-ho-l-ni-hi n-da-l-nish go-ne-e	da-na-eh be-hus-on-ge	ol-ta-bi-na- ta-nee	chay-ji- ja-go

Schedule	Secretary	Tardy	Teacher
8:30 Welcome/Class Business			
9:00 Language Arts			
10:30 Mathematics			
11:30 Social Studies			
12:00 Lunch			
1:00 Science			
2:00 Art/Music/PE			
Oo'áál bik'ehgo e'elínígíí	**Naaltsoos ałkéé' neinilí**	**Doo hąhda yah ajííyá**	**Bá ólta'í**
o-al bi-ke-go e-el-i-ni-gee	na-l-sos a-l-kay nay-ni-li	do hah-da ya a-jee-ya	ba-ol-ta-i

Assignment Words: Class Dictionary

Assignment	Correct	Design	Directions
Ádoolníílígíí	**T'áá ákót'é**	**Bik'ehgo ni'dooch'ąh**	**Bik'ehgo á'doolnííł**
a-do-l-neel-i-gi	ta a-ko-tay	bi-ke-go ni-do-cha	bi-ke-go a-do-neel
To Discuss	To Draw	Due Date	Grade
Baa yá'áti'	**Na'ach'ąąh**	**Hagho ádoolníílígíí**	**Hait'áo ihoo'ą́ą́'**
ba ya-ti-i	na-a-cha	hah-go a-dol-neel-i-gee	hay-ta-o i-ho-a
To Help	Homework	To Listen	Permission Letter
Áká a'ayeed	**Hooghandi ádoolníílígíí**	**Ajíísts'ą́ą́'**	**Naaltsoos bee łá dooleełígíí**
a-ka a-a-yay-d	ho-gan-di a-do-neel-i-gee	a-jees-sa	na-l-sos bay la do-lay-li-gee
Questions	To Read	Stop	To Take Notes
Na'ídíkid	**Wolta'**	**K'adí**	**Naaltsoos bikáá' ájílééh**
na-i-di-kid	wol-ta	ka-di	na-l-sos bi-ka a-ji-lee
Test	To Turn In	To Write	Wrong
Bee na'antá	**Yah análtzóóz**	**Ak'e'elchí**	**Doo ákót'ée da**
bay na-an-ta	ya-a-nal-sos	a-ke-el-chi	do a-ko-tay da

Playground and Physical Education Vocabulary: Class Dictionary

Ball	Baseball	Basketball	To Catch
Jooł	**Jóół yikalí**	**Jooł iihnálniihí**	**Bił jidideeł**
jol	jol yi-kal-i	jol ee-na-nil-i	bil ji-di-day-l

To Change	Circle	Drill	Field
Éé łahgo át'éhígíí bííh jighááh	**Názbas**	**Óhoo'aah**	**Jooł bee na'anéégi**
ee-la-go a-te-hi-gee bee ji-ga	naz-bas	o-hoo-aa	jol bay na-a-ne-gi

To Follow	Football (American)	Four Square	Go in Front
Bikéé' joogááł	**Jooł yitalí**	**Dii dika'**	**Alaaji'aninaah**
bi-kay jo-gal	jol yi-tal-i	dii-deki	alaagy-knee-neh-nah

Gym Clothes	Handball	To Hit	Hurt
Na'a'né bi'éé'	**Jooł'nabiznilgaati**	**Nízhdiiłghaał**	**Neezgai**
na-a-ne bi-ay	jol-nabiz-nil-cod-di	nish-deel-hal	nay-z-gay

To Jump	Jumprope	Kickball	Line
Dahnázhníljį́į́h	**Tlool' ba'dah'neejii'chei**	**Jooł'yitali**	**Jinít'i'**
da-nash-nil-jee	klil-bada-ne-ji-chei-eh	jol-ye-tal-e	ji-ni-ti

Lock	Locker Room	To Lose	Out of Bounds
Bil dah ná'át'áhí	**Tá'adazhdigis góne'**	**Hwaa honeezná**	**Asdzoh bilááhdi**
bil da na-ta-hi	ta-a-daz-di-gis go-ne	wha ho-nay-z-na	as-zo bi-la-di
The Rules	To Run	Shoes	Sideline
Bik'ehgo na'a'né	**Joolwoł**	**Ké**	**Nidajinéh bąąhgi**
bi-ke-go e-e-l-i	jol-wol	ke	ni-da ji-nay ba-gi
Soccer	Sport	To Stretch	Team
Jooł yitalí	**Daané'é**	**Na'ízhdílts'ǫǫd**	**Ałch'odaji'níigo**
jol yi-tal-i	da-ne-e	na-ish-dil-sod	al-cho-da-ji-nee-go
Tetherball	To Throw	Volleyball	Whistle
Tlool' jool	**Ahilghan**	**Jóół nabízníkaadí**	**Bee ázdísoolí**
jol-klil-ba-dasi-ah	a-hil-han	jol na-biz-ni-ka-di	bay az-di-sol-i

Science Vocabulary: Class Dictionary

Acid	Animal	Base	Climate
Tó adiłidí to a-di-li-di	**Naaldlooshii** na-l-o-shee	**Tó niłtólí** to nil-to-li	**Áhoot'éhígíí** a-ho-te-hi-gee
Dinosaur	Earth	Electricity	Energy
Tł'ish tsoh tl-ish soh	**Na'hasd'zaan** na-has-zhan	**Atsi'nil'tlish** at-si-nil-clis	**Ayol** a-yol
Environment	Experiment	Extinct	Hypothesis
Nahasdzáán bikáá' áhoot'éhígíí na-has-zan bi-ka a-ho-tay-hi-gee	**Naalkaah nabóhonítaah** na-l-ka na-bo-hon-i-taa	**Ásdįįd** as-deed	**Sha'shin hwiinidzinígíí** sha-shin hee-ni-zin-i-gee
To Investigate	Lab Notebook	Laboratory	Matter
Naal kei na-al-ki-ei	**Naaltsoos bik'ehgo niji nishígíí** nat-sos bi-ke-go ni-jil-nish-i-gee	**Na'alkaah góne'** na-al-ka go-ne	**Taa doole'e bee'hadit'ei** ta-do-la-ei be hadi-tah
Motion	Planet	Plant	Science
Naha'ná na-ha-nah	**Yádiłhił bii' kéyah dah naaznilígíí** ya-dil-hil bee ke-ya da naz-nil-i-gii	**Ch'il** chil	**Na'alkaah dóó éé'deetįįh bił haz'áájí** na-al-ka do ay-day-ti bil haz-a-ji

Math Vocabulary: Class Dictionary

To Add	Answer	To Calculate	Calculator
Ahiihi'nííł a-hee-hi-neel	$1 + 1 = 2$ **Díkwíí yileehígíí** di-kw-ee yi-lay-i-gii	$\begin{array}{r} 7 \\ 8 \\ +5 \\ \hline 20 \end{array}$ **Díkwíí yileehígíí** di-kw-ee	**Námboo neizooígíí** nam-bo nay-zoo-i-gee
To Combine	To Divide	Equation	Exponent
Ahiihi'nííł a-hi-hi-neel	$\div$ **Ałtsá'nííł** al-sa-neel	$2 + 3 = 5$ **Díkwíí yileehígíí** di-kw-ee	A^4 **Exponent** ex-po-nent
Graph	Math	To Multiply	Numbers
Na'asdzoh na-as-zo	**Ahiihi'nííł dóó ałtsádzoh** a-hi-hi-neel do al-sa-zoh	3×2 **Ahááh náhideeł** a-ha na-hee-deel	$1\ 2\ 3\ 4\ 5$ $6\ 7\ 8\ 9$ **Námboo** nam-bo
To Order	Problem	Property	To Prove
$1, 2, 3, 4$ **Ałkéé'nii'nííł** al-kay-nee-neel	$1 + 3 = ?$ **Bóhwiintaah nabidíkidígíí** bo-wheen-ta na-bi-di-kid-i-gee	$x(y + 2)$ **Bits'áadóó** bi-sa do	**íishjání álnééh** eesh ja-ni a-l-ne
To Simplify	To Solve	To Subtract	Variable
$\frac{3X + 42}{4} = 6X \longrightarrow X = 2$ **Bee hózinigo ályaa** bee-ho-zi-ni-go al-yaa	$3x = 12$ $X = 4$ **Díkwíí yileehígíí** di-kwee yi-lay-i-gee	$12 - 6$ **Bitsá'nííł** bi-sa-neel	x, y **Bee na'nitaah** bay na-ni-ta

Social Studies Vocabulary: Class Dictionary

Africa	Asia	Australia	Buddhist
Naakai łizhinii bikéyah	**Náá'áłts'ózí bikéyah**	**Na'hashte'iitsoh bikéyah**	**Buddhist**
na-kay li-shin-ee bi-ke-ya	na-al-so-si bi-ke-ya	na-has-te-tso bi-ke-ya	bood-hist
Christian	Citizenship	Continent	Country
Oodlání	**Iliigo keyah bil keedahojitiinii**	**Kéyah dah naaznilígíí**	**Kéyah danitsaágíí**
o-la-ni	e-leego-keyah-beka-ge-ke-hoji-tei	ke-ya da naz-nil-i-gee	ke-ya da-ni-sa-i-gee
Democracy	Europe	Geography	Government
Dine'beenah'atei bee'bo'holniih	**To'anaanídi Bilagáana bikéyah**	**Kéyah dah naaznil bíł haz'áníjí**	**Waashindoon si'a'**
dine' beenah-ha-tah ba-bohol-neh	to-a-naa-ni-di Bila-gah-na bi-ke-ya	ke-ya da naz-nil bil haz-a-ni-ji	washin-doon si-ah
Hinduism	History	Jewish	Map
Keyah India Dine' be'oodla dilzinii	**Alk'idáá' ádahoodzaa yéé baa hane'**	**Jewish**	**Keyah naaltsoos bikáá' be'elyaa**
keyah-india-holyadi-be-odla-dil-zin-ni	al-kid-a a-da-ho-za ye ba ha-ne	jew-ish	ke-ya na-l-sos bi-ka be-el-ya
Muslim	North American	South America	World
Muslim	**Náhookǫsjí kéyah dah si'ánígíí**	**Shádi'ááhjí kéyah dah si'ánígíí**	**Nahasdzáán dah si'ánígíí**
mu-sel-im	na-ho-kos-ji ke-ya da si-a-ni-gee	sha-di-a-ji ke-ya da si-a-ni-gee sha-di-a-ji	na-ha-san da si-a-ni-gee

Welcome to My Classroom

Dear Parent or Guardian,

I would like to welcome your child to my classroom. The first couple of weeks can be difficult for students who don't yet speak English, but by working with you as a team I hope to make the transition as smooth as possible. While my Navajo is not strong, I will do the best I can to communicate what is expected of your child in the classroom and in the school. Please feel free to stop by before or just after school, or to call anytime.

Again, welcome to our school! I look forward to speaking with you soon.

Sincerely,

Amá dóó azhé'é,

Ne'awéé' yá'át'eeh bidideeshniił. Áłtse ha'altááhgo áláahdi nantł'ah łeh áłchíní doo Bilagáana k'ehjí yádaałti'ígíí bá, ndi ahił ndeilnishgo hozhó'ó ne'awéé' í dínóóldįįł. Doo hózhó'óó diné k'ehjí yáshti' da ndi ne'awéé' hait'áo nizhónígo ajółta' łehígíí bee bił hashne' dooleeł. Ólta'di deesháá́ł nínízingo t'áá ako t'ah doo ha'altáágóó éí doodago ch'íjíjahgo bikéé'dóó, éí doodago shich'į' hodíílnih. Yá'ánáánát'ééh. Nił nááháshne' doolééł át'ah.

Hágoónee',

Your Child Is a Pleasure to Have in Class

Dear Parent or Guardian,

This is a note of thanks to let you know that your child is a pleasure to have in class and to thank you for the work you do at home to help your child succeed. Though your child sometimes has difficulties with the language, he or she is trying hard and making progress every day. Keep up the good work!

Sincerely,

Amá dóó azhé'é,

Díí éí t'óó ahéhee' nidideeshniił nisin ne'awéé' shá ółta'ígíí. Azhą shı̨́ı̨́ łahda saad bił nantł'ah łeh ndi t'áá akwíí jí yidiil'ą́ dóó yi hooł'aahdo. Nizhónígo bił nanilnishgo.

Hágoónee',

Your Child Is Not Performing Up to Ability

Dear Parent or Guardian,

Though your child is smart and capable, he or she is not performing up to his or her ability. We understand that it's difficult to learn when you don't speak the language, but the only way to learn is to try, and your child needs to try harder. If you have any questions, please stop by before or just after school, or give me a call anytime.

Sincerely,

Amá dóó azhé'é,

Ne'awéé' ayóó t'áádoo le'é bił bééhózin dóó yíneel'ąa ndi doo yéego yinaalnish da. T'áá aníí saad doo hwił bééhózingóó ayóó nantł'ah łeh íhwiizhdooł'áálgo, ndi t'áá bízhnootįįłgo t'éíyá ákó ne'awéé yéego naalnishgo t'éíyá á'doonííł. Na'ídíkid nee hólǫ́ǫ́go shaa díínááł, éí doodago shich'į' hodííłnih.

Hágoónéé',

Please Schedule a Meeting

Dear Parent or Guardian,

Please call or stop by the school office to schedule a meeting concerning your child. We understand that your time is valuable, but this is very important.

Sincerely,

Amá dóó azhé'é,

Shich'i' hodíílnih éí doodago nihaa díínááł dóó bee nih dooł'ááł ne'awéé baa áłah diidleeł̨gíí. Ninaanish shį̨į́ hólǫo ndi, díí aláahdi bá baa nitsáhákees.

Hágoónee',

I am the parent of _____.

Shí éí _____. **bimá nish doo bizhe'e niidlį̨.**

❑ I need a translator.

❑ **Ata' halne'í ła' nisin ákwe'é naagháa doo.**

Your Child's Behavior Is a Problem

Dear Parent or Guardian,

Your child's behavior is unacceptable. Not only does your child create an environment where he or she cannot learn, but your child is also disrupting the learning of others. I hope we can work as a team to help your child learn to behave appropriately in school. If your child continues his or her current behavior, it will result in severe disciplinary action. If you have any questions, please stop by before or just after school, or give me a call anytime.

Sincerely,

Amá dóó azhé'é,

Ne'awéé' be'ádíláhígíí éí doo bee báhaz'ą̧ą da. Áłchíní biniinaa doo ídahooł'aah da. Hozhó'ó ahił ndeilnishgo ne'awéé' ndadíníítį̧ į̧ ł ólta'di. T'áá ákót'įį́go éí yéégo naaltsoos bee ndooltsos. Na'ídíkid nee hólǫ̧ǫgo shaa díínááł éí doodago shich'į' hodíílnih.

Hágoónee',

Absences Are Hurting Performance

Dear Parent or Guardian,

Your child's absences are hurting his or her performance. Much of what we do in school builds on what we did the day before; if a student is absent it can be very hard to catch up. I hope that we can work together as a team to help make sure that your child attends class. If you have any questions, please stop by before or just after school, or give me a call anytime.

Sincerely,

Amá dóó azhé'é,

Ne'awéé' ólta' niyiisíhígíí bee bóhodiit'į́ biníínah doo ha'zho'ó e'elį́įda. T'áá kwííjį́ olta'di ada'į́įlínígíí éi binahjí ínaahoo' aah baa neikaiígíí ałkee'sinilgo bíhoo'aahgo baa neikai; ólta' niyiisi hgo t'áą́' ninábiiłt'eeh. Ahił neilnishgo shį́į́ ne'awéé' biká adiijah hozhó'ó ólta' dooleeł. Na'ídíkid nee hólǫ́ǫgo shaa díínááł éí doo dago olta'ii chi'níjeehgo da éí doodago shich'į' hodíílnih.

Hágoónéé',

Tardiness Is Hurting Performance

Dear Parent or Guardian,

Your child is frequently late to class, and this tardiness is hurting his or her performance. By missing the beginning of the period, your child misses important directions and information, making it impossible for him or her to keep up with the rest of the class. I hope that we can work together as a team to help make sure that your child attends class. If you have any questions, please stop by before or just after school, or give me a call anytime.

Sincerely,

Amá dóó azhé'é,

Ne'awéé' ayóó ólta'di doo hahda nádááh dóó akéédę́ę́ nídinidleeh bits'ą́ądóó bee nít'į́. Ólta' hahalzhishgo jiisihgo t'áádoo le'é lą'í baa dahane' dóó bídahoo'aah dóó díí nát'ą́ą́ kóbósin. Ahił nei nishgo shį́į́ ne'awéé' hozhó'ó ólta' dooleeł. Na'ídíkid nee hólǫ́ǫgo shaa díínááł éí doodago shich'į' hodíílnih.

Hágoónéé',

General Resources That School Offers

Dear Parent or Guardian,

The teachers and staff here at school hope to help you and your child in any way we can. The school offers translators and may also be able to help with school supplies and other services. Please feel free to stop by the school office anytime to explore the services available. If you work during the day, you can always call or send a note with your child. We hope to talk to you soon!

Sincerely,

Amá dóó azhé'é,

Bá'ólta'í danilínígíí dóó kwe'é ndaalnishígíí níká adiijah dan ízin. Ólta' éí ná ata'hodoolnihígíí la' bee dahóló̜ dóó ólta' biniiyé chodao'ínígíí yee níká adoojahgo át'é. Nihaa díínaał łahda dóó díí bee níká 'a'dóówołígíí baa ndíníítaał. Jí̜igo nanilnishgo éí nihich'i̜' hodíílnih éí doodago naaltsoos bikáá' ádíílíílgo ne'awéé' baa dííłtsos. Át'ah shí̜í̜ ahił náá hwiilne' dooleeł.

Hágoónee',

11

Reading Tests

The native language reading tests included in this book are very basic tools that can help you make educated guesses about a student's reading level and possibly about his or her prior schooling. These do not replace the more detailed assessments that will be administered by your district's ELL services, but they will allow you to troubleshoot your ELL students' instruction until these services are put in place. The included tests are simplified versions of the Running Reading Records that many teachers use to assess reading fluency in English-speaking students.

How to use these tests:

- Have a student read for one minute, following the text with his or her finger.
- You will not be able to understand the student's language, but even in an unfamiliar language, you will be able to tell if a student is reading fluently or is stumbling. Expect reading levels to vary from language to language (a Chinese newspaper contains about 3,000 different characters!); look generally for students' reading ease, rather than defining a number of words that a student must reach in order to "pass."
- At the end of one minute, evaluate the student's general reading ability.

Use these tests to:

- Decide what reading level of translated material you will request from your district's ELL services (or find in the library or online).
- Aid in evaluating a student's prior exposure to literacy.

- Determine how you will use the resources of this book. If the student can read in his or her native language, he or she will be able to use this book's dictionaries with more independence.
- Evaluate the strategies you will use to help the student learn English. If the student is literate in his or her native language, you may decide to use printed materials such as phrasebooks and dictionaries rather than oral language drills.
- Choose instructional strategies—should this student be reading for content, or should he or she be focusing on basic literacy?

The Little Cat

One day I saw a little cat. It lived behind Ms. White's house. The cat came out to greet me. It rubbed against my leg. I stroked the cat and it purred.

The next day I saw the cat again. It followed me all the way to school. When it was time to go home, the cat was still there. I walked past Ms. White's house, but the cat kept following me.

When I got home my mom was surprised. She gave the cat some milk in a dish. The cat liked the milk. I named the cat Pumpkin.

The next day, I stopped at Ms. White's house. I asked her about Pumpkin. Ms. White said that it was not her cat. She thought the cat could use a good home.

Now Pumpkin lives at my house but he still follows me to school every day.

The Little Cat: Spanish

El Gatito

Un día vi un gatito, que vivía detrás de la casa de la Sra. Blanca. El gato salió a saludarme y se frotó contra mi pierna. Lo acaricié y ronroneó.

El día siguiente vi al gato otra vez. Me siguió hasta la escuela. Cuándo salí de la escuela, el gato todavía estaba allí. Pasé por la casa de la Sra. Blanca, pero el gato me siguió.

Cundo llegué a casa mi mamá se sorprendió. Le dio leche en un plato y le gustó. Lo llamé Calabaza.

Al día siguiente, pasé por la casa de la Sra. Blanca para preguntarle sobre Calabaza. La Sra. Blanca me dijo que no era su gato y pensó que le vendría bien un hogar.

Ahora Calabaza vive en mi casa, pero todavía me sigue a la escuela cada día.

The Little Cat: Vietnamese

Con Meøo Nhoû

Một ngày nọ tôi thấy có một con mèo nhỏ. Nó sống ở đằng sau nhà của Cô White. Nó bước ra để chào tôi, cà thân mình nó vào chân tôi. Tôi vuốt ve nó và nó kêu ừ . . . ừ.

Hôm sau tôi lại nhìn thấy nó. Nó theo suốt tôi trên đường đến trường. Khi đến giờ ra về, con mèo vẫn còn ở đó. Tôi đi qua ngôi nhà của Cô White nhưng nó vẫn tiếp tục đi theo tôi.

Khi tôi về đến nhà thì mẹ tôi rất ngạc nhiên. Bà cho nó một ít sữa trong cái đĩa. Nó rất thích sữa. Tôi tên đặt tên cho nó là Bí Đỏ.

Ngày hôm sau, tôi ghé qua nhà cô White và hỏi cô về con Bí Đỏ. Cô White cho biết con mèo đó không phải của cô. Cô nghĩ có thể là nó cần một nơi ở tốt.

Giờ đây Bí Đỏ đã ở trong nhà của tôi nhưng vẫn theo sau tôi mỗi ngày đến trường.

The Little Cat: Hmong

Tus Miv Me Me

Muaj ib hnub kuv pom ib tug miv me me. Nws nyob nraum Niam Ntxawm White qaum tsev. Tus miv tawm tuaj tos kuv. Nws muab nws lub cev tshiav kuv txhais ceg. Kuv plhws tus miv ces nws nqus pob.

Tag kis kuv rov pom tus miv dua. Nws lawv kuv qab mus txog tom tsev kawm ntawv. Thaum txog caij los tsev, tus miv tseem nyob ntawd thiab. Kuv los dhau Niam Ntxawm White lub tsev lawm los tus miv tseem pheej lawv kuv qab qees.

Thaum kuv los txog tsev ua rau kuv niam ceeb nkaus. Nws hliv mis nyuj rau hauv ib lub tais ces muab rau tus miv haus. Tus miv nyiam mis nyuj kawg li. Kuv muab nws tis npe hu ua Taub.

Tag kis, kuv tau nres ntawm Niam Ntxawm White lub tsev. Kuv nug nws txog Taub. Niam Ntxawm White hais tias tsis yog nws tus miv. Nws xav tias tej zaum tus miv yuav tau ib lub zoo tsev nyob.

Niam no Taub los nyob hauv kuv lub tsev lawm tab sis nws tseem niaj hnub lawv kuv qab mus tom tsev kawm ntawv.

The Little Cat: Traditional Chinese Script

小貓

有一天，我看到一隻小貓。它住在懷特小姐的家後頭。小貓跑出來迎接我。它磨蹭我的腿。我撫摸小貓，它發出滿足的呼嚕呼嚕聲。

第二天我又看到小貓。它一路跟著我到學校。到了回家的時候，小貓還是在那裡。我走過懷特小姐的家，可是小貓繼續跟著我。

當我回到家時，媽媽很驚訝。她在小碟子中倒了一點牛奶給小貓吃。小貓很喜歡　牛奶。我給小貓取了一個名字叫「南瓜」。

第二天，我到懷特小姐的家。我詢問有關於「南瓜」的事。懷特小姐說　「南瓜」不是她的貓。她覺得小貓有一個能夠照顧它的家是一件好事。

現在，「南瓜」住在我的家，可是它每天還是照常跟著我到學校。

The Little Cat: Korean

작은 고양이

어느날 나는 작은 고양이 한마리를 보았습니다. 고양이는 미스 화이트 집 뒷쪽에 살고 있었습니다. 작은 고양이는 달려나와서 나를 맞이하였습니다. 그리고 내 다리에 비벼대었습니다. 고양이를 어루만지니까 고양이가 가르랑 소리를 내었습니다.

다음 날 나는 작은 고양이를 또 봤습니다. 고양이는 학교까지 나를 따라왔습니다. 집에 갈 시간이 되었을 때도 고양이는 거기에 있었습니다. 나는 미스 화이트 집을 지나쳤지만 고양이는 계속해서 나를 따라왔습니다.

내가 집에 도착했을 때 엄마는 놀라셨습니다. 엄마는 작은 접시에 우유를 부어서 고양이에게 먹였습니다. 고양이는 우유를 참 좋아했습니다. 나는 고양이에게 '펌킨'이라는 이름을 지어주었습니다.

다음 날 나는 미스 화이트 집에 갔습니다. 나는 미스 화이트에게 펌킨에 대해 물어봤습니다. 미스 화이트는 펌킨이 자신의 고양이가 아니라고 말했습니다. 그리고 고양이를 돌봐줄 수 있는 집이 있는 것은 고양이에게 참 좋은 일이라고 말했습니다.

이제 펌킨은 우리 집에 살고 있습니다. 하지만 여전히 매일 나를 따라서 학교에 갑니다.

The Little Cat: Haitian Creole

Ti chat la

Yon jou mwen te wè yon ti chat. Li te abite dèyè kay madmwazèl White. Chat la te sòti vin salye m. Li fwote kò l sou janm mwen. Mwen te karese chat la epi li te myole.

Nan landmen mwen te wè chat la ankò. Li te swiv mwen jiskaske mwen te rive lekòl la. Lè li te lè pou m al lakay mwen, chat la te toujou la. Mwen mache depase kay madmwazèl White, men chat la kontinye pouswiv mwen.

Lè mwen te rive lakay, manman m te sezi. Li te bay chat la yon ti lèt nan yon veso. Chat la te renmen lèt la. Mwen te rele chat la Pumpkin (Sitwouy).

Nan landmen, men pase lakay madmwazèl White. Mwen mande l pou Pumpkin. Madmwazèl White te di m konsa se pa pou li chat la ye. Li te panse chat la ka bezwen yon bon kay.

Kounye a Pumpkin abite lakay mwen men li toujou swiv mwen lè m pral lekòl chak jou.

The Little Cat: Arabic

القطة الصغيرة

تعيش خلف منزل مسز "واي . خرجت القطة للخارج لترحب بـ
بيدي على القطة وآنت مسرورة . في يو م ما ، رأيت قطة صغيرة.
إحتكت القطة بساقي . مررت

أخرى . تبعتني القطة طول الطريق إلى المدرسة . وعندما حان الوقت
مسز "وايت" ولكنالقطة تبعتني . وفي اليوم التالي، رأيت القطة مرة
للرجوع إلى المنزل، آنت هي بإنتظاري. مررت على منزل

مندهشة. أعطت أمي للقطة قليل من اللبن في طبق ، القطة لعقت اللبن.
"بامبك". أنا سميت القطة و عندما وصلت إلى المنزل، أمي آنت

". وسألت عن "بامبكن ". قالت لي مسز " وايد القطة " انها لاتملك
منزل جيد لتعيش فيه . وفي اليوم التالي، توقفت عند منزل مسز "وايت
القطة . وهي تعتقد بأن القطة تحتاج إلى

بامبكن " الآن في منزلي ولكنها مازالت آل يوم إلى المدرسة.
". "تعيش"

The Little Cat: Russian

Котёнок

Однажды я увидел котёнка. Он жил за домом Мисс Уайт. Он вышел ко мне навстречу и потёрся о мою ногу. Я погладил котёнка, и он замурлыкал.

На следующий день я вновь увидел котёнка. Он проводил меня до школы. Когда подошло время возвращаться домой, котёнок ждал меня на том же месте. Я прошел мимо дома Мисс Уайт, но котёнок продолжал бежать за мной.

Дома мама очень удивилась. Она налила котёнку немного молока в блюдце. Котёнку молоко понравилось. Я назвал его Тыковка.

На следующий день я зашёл к Мисс Уайт и спросил её про Тыковку. Но Мисс Уайт сказала, что это не её котенок и что ему нужен хороший хозяин.

Теперь Тыковка живёт у нас и каждый день провожает меня в школу.

The Little Cat: Tagalog
Ang Maliit na Pusa

Isang araw, nakakita ako ng isang maliit na pusa. Nakatira ito sa likuran ng bahay ni Bb. White. Lumabas ang pusa upang batiin ako. Ikinuskos nito ang katawan sa aking binti. Hinagod ko ang pusa at ito ay ngumiyaw.

Nang sumunod na araw ay nakita kong muli ang pusa. Ito ay sumunod sa akin hanggang sa paaralan. Nang oras na para umuwi, ang pusa ay naroroon pa rin. Dumaan ako sa bahay ni Bb. White, pero patuloy na sumunod sa akin ang pusa.

Nang makarating ako sa bahay ay nagulat ang aking ina. Binigyan niya ang pusa ng gatas sa mangkok. Nagustuhan ng pusa ang gatas. Pinangalanan ko ang pusa ng Pumpkin.

Nang sumunod na araw, pumunta ako sa bahay ni Bb. White. Nagtanong ako sa kanya tungkol kay Pumpkin. Sinabi ni Bb. White na ito ay hindi niya pusa. Sa palagay niya ay kailangan ng pusa ang isang mabuting tahanan.

Ngayon ay nakatira si Pumpkin sa aming bahay pero sinusundan pa rin niya ako patungo sa paaralan araw-araw.

The Little Cat: Navajo

Mósí Yázhí

Łah mósí yázhí léí' yiiłtsą. Ms. White bighan bine'jí bighan. Shich'į' ch'íníyá. Shijáád yé'nah ńt'éé'. Bídíshnihgo ání.

Biskání mósí náánééłtsą. Ólta'góó shikéé' níyá. Ch'íniijéé'go t'ahdii sidá. Ms. White bighan bííghah dahdiiyá ndi t'áá shikéé' yigááł.

Hooghandi nánísdzáago shimá yik'ee deesyiz. Mósí abe' łeets'aa' bigigo yee níką. Mósí abe' bił łikan. Pumpkin bidííniid.

Biiskání Ms. White bighandi níyá. Pumpkin bínábídééłkid. Doo shí shimósí da ní Ms. White. Mósí shíį́ nizhónígo hooghan bee hodooleeł ní.

K'ad Pumpkin shighandi bighan ndi t'áá kwíí jį́ ólta'góó shikéé' ałnánálwo'.

Bird Nest

Have you ever watched birds build a nest? I have.

First, they find a good tree branch. The tree branch has to be high enough so that people can't reach it and big enough so that it won't break in a storm.

Then they gather sticks and pieces of cloth from all over town. You might have seen birds flying with things in their beaks. These birds are probably building a nest.

The next step is to weave the sticks together. They shove one stick here and another stick there and soon they have a nest. But it is not done yet! Next, the birds have to line the nest with soft things like cloth or fur. Some birds even decorate their nest with shiny things.

Now the nest is almost finished. There is only one more thing this nest needs. What do you think it is?

If you guessed eggs, then you were right. When the bird lays eggs in the nest, then it is finished.

Bird Nest: Spanish

El Nido del Pájaro

¿Has visto a pájaros construyendo un nido? Yo sí.

Primero, eligen una buena rama, la cual tiene que ser lo suficientemente alta para que las personas no la puedan alcanzar y suficientemente grande para que no se rompa durante una tormenta.

Después recogen ramitas y pedazos de tela por todas partes del pueblo. Es posible que hayas visto pájaros que llevan cosas en el pico. Estos pájaros probablemente están construyendo un nido.

El próximo paso es entretejer las ramitas. Ponen una ramita aquí y otra allá y de pronto tienen un nido. ¡Pero ahí no termina todavía! Los pájaros tienen que forrar el nido con cosas suaves como tela o piel. Algunos pájaros incluso decoran su nido con cosas brillantes.

El nido ya casi está terminado. Sólo le hace falta una cosa. ¿Qué crees que sea?

Si pensaste en los huevos, entonces tienes razón. Cuando el pájaro pone sus huevos en el nido, éste queda terminado.

Bird Nest: Vietnamese

Tổ chim

Các em có bao giờ nhìn thấy chim xây tổ chưa? Tôi đã nhìn thấy rồi đấy.

Đầu tiên, chúng tìm một nhánh cây thích hợp. Nhánh cây phải đủ cao để con người không đụng tới được và đủ lớn để không bị gãy đổ trong cơn mưa bão.

Sau đó, chúng nhặt nhạnh các mẩu cây nhỏ và những mảnh vải từ khắp nơi trong thành phố. Chắc các em đã nhìn thấy chúng ngậm cái gì đó trong mỏ khi đang bay. Chắc chắn những con chim này đang xây tổ.

Bước tiếp theo là chúng kết những mẩu cây này lại. Chúng nhét một mẩu cây ở chỗ này và mẩu kia ở chỗ khác và chẳng bao lâu sau thì tạo nên một cái tổ. Nhưng vẫn chưa xong đâu! Kế đến chúng lót tổ bằng những thứ mềm như vải hay lông thú. Thậm chí có những con còn trang hoàng tổ của chúng bằng những thứ sáng bóng.

Giờ thì tổ đã gần như hoàn tất. Chỉ còn cần duy nhất một thứ nữa thôi. Các em có biết đó là gì không?

Nếu các em đoán đó là những quả trứng thì đúng rồi đó. Khi chim đẻ trứng trong tổ thì đã xong rồi.

Bird Nest: Hmong

Zes Noog

Koj puas tau pom noog ua zes dua? Kuv pom dua lawm.

Lawv xub nrhiav kom tau ib tug ceg ntoo. Tus ceg ntoo yuav tsum nyob qhov siab txaus kom neeg ncav tsis cuag thiab loj txaus kom cua ntaus tsis lov.

Dhau ntawd lawv mam sau khaub thiab sau khaub hlab raws qab vag tsib taug. Tej zaum koj yuav pom noog kwv khaub ya. Cov noog ua li no tej zaum yog lawv ua zes.

Lawv xub xub pib muab cov khaub los sib khaum ua ke. Lawv tso ib tug khaub rau ntawm no lwm tus khaub rau tod, tsis ntev ces ua tau zoo li lub zes lawm. Tab sis tsis tau tiav tiag tiag! Dhau ntawd, tus noog yuav tsum nrhiav tej yam mos mos zoo xws li ntaub los plaub los ua rau qhov kawg. Muaj ib txhia noog lawv tseem txawj nrhiav tej yam ci ci los ua kom lawv lub zes zoo nkauj.

Tam sis no lub zes yuav luag tiav lawm. Tab sis tshuav ib yam kom yuav tsum muaj nyob rau hauv lub zes. Koj xav tias yuav yog dab tsi?

Yog koj twv tias yog qe, ces koj teb yog lawm. Thaum noog nteg qe rau hauv lawm ces lub zes thiaj tag lawm tiag.

Bird Nest: Traditional Chinese Script

鳥巢

你有沒有看過鳥在築巢？我有。

首先，它們會找一個很好的樹枝。樹枝的高度要高到讓人夠不著，還要大到能夠經受住暴風雨的襲擊。

然後，它們從城鎮的各個角落收集枝條和碎布片。你可能看過鳥在嘴中含著東西飛翔。這些鳥很可能是在築巢。

下一個步驟是把枝條編排在一起。它們把一根枝條插到這裡，把另一根枝條插到那裡，不久，就築好一個巢。但是這樣還不算大功告成！下一步，鳥需要用柔軟的東西，像碎布片或軟毛之類爲巢鋪上襯墊。有些鳥甚至用閃亮的東西裝飾 它們的巢。

到這裡，可以說幾乎蓋好巢了。現在，這個巢只差一樣東西。你想那一樣 東西是什麼？

如果你的回答是「蛋」，那麼你就答對了。當鳥在巢中下蛋，築巢就此完成了。

Bird Nest: Korean

새 둥지

새가 둥지를 만드는 것을 본 적이 있나요? 저는 본 적이 있습니다.

새들은 우선 좋은 나뭇가지를 찾습니다. 나뭇가지의 높이는 사람이 닿을 수 없을 정도로 높아야 하고 폭풍우에도 부러지지 않을 정도로 커야 합니다.

그리고 나서 동네 곳곳에서 작은 나뭇 조각들과 천을 수집해 옵니다. 여러분은 아마도 새들이 입에 뭔가를 물고 날으는 것을 본 적이 있을 것입니다. 그 새들은 어쩌면 둥지를 짓고 있었을 것입니다.

다음 단계는 작은 나뭇 조각들을 엮는 것입니다. 새들은 나뭇 조각 하나를 이쪽으로 끼우고, 또 다른 하나를 저쪽으로 끼우고 해서 얼마 지나지 않아 둥지를 완성합니다. 하지만 여기에서 끝나는 것이 아닙니다! 그 다음엔 천이나 털과 같은 부드러운 물건으로 둥지를 채웁니다. 어떤 새들은 심지어 반짝이는 물건으로 둥지를 장식하기도 합니다.

자 이제 둥지가 거의 다 완성되어 갑니다. 오직 한 가지만 있으면 됩니다. 그게 뭘까요?

'알'이라고 생각했다면 정답입니다. 새가 둥지에 알을 낳으면 둥지 짓기는 그때서야 비로소 완성된 것이랍니다.

Bird Nest: Haitian Creole

Nich zwazo

Èske w pa janm konn gade yon zwazo k ap bati yon nich ? Mwen te wè sa.

Toudabò, yo jwenn yon bon branch bwa. Branch bwa a dwe ase wo pou moun paka rive ladan l epi li dwe ase gwo pou l pa kraze lè gen yon tanpèt.

Answit yo ranmase ti mose bwa ak moso twal toupatou nan zòn nan. Ou ka konn wè zwazo k ap vole avèk kèk bagay nan bèk yo. Petèt se yon nich zwazo sa yo ap bati.

Pwochen etap la se pou tise moso bwa yo ansanm. Yo pouse yon ti moso bwa isi e la epi anvan lontan yon gen yon nich. Men li poko fini ! Answit, zwazo a gen pou l double nich lan ak bagay ki soup tankou twal oswa fouri. Gen kèk zwazo ki menm dekore nich yo avèk bagay ki klere.

Kounye a nich lan prèske fini. Genyen yon sèl lòt bagay nich lan bezwen. Ki sa w panse li ye ?

Si w te devine ze, ou gen rezon. Lè zwazo a ponn ze nan nich lan, se lè sa a li fini.

Bird Nest: Arabic

عش العصفور

هل شاهدت عصفو ًاريبيني عشا؟ نعم.

لابد أن يكون فرع الشجرة عالي الإرتفاع حتي لا يستطيع أحد من
لا ينكسر خلال العاصفة . أولا، لابد أن العصافير فرع شجرة جيد.
الناس أن يصل اليه ، ولابد أن يكون الفرع قوي حتي

وقطع من القماش من آل انحاء المدينة. من المحتمل أن تكون قد رأيت
تلك الطيور غالباًتبني عش . وبعد ، آ ان عليهم أن يجمعوا العصي
عصافير محلقة في الجو وتحمل أشياء في مناقيرها.

ببعض. يدفعون عصا من هنا وعصا من هناك وقريبا سيكو ن لديهم
عش ولكن لم ينته بعد! الخطوة التالية هي تشبيك العصي بعضها
على العصفور تبطين العش بإشياء ناعمة مثل قطع القماش أو الفراء.
تزين بعض العصافير عشها بإشياء لامعة. وبعد ذلك ، يجب

العش الآن على وشك الإآتمال. هناك شيء واحد يحتاجه هذا العش.
سيكون

ماذا تعتعقد بأن يكون هذا الشيء؟

. وعندما العصفور يبيض في العش عندئذ يكون العش قد آتمل .
إذا اعتقدت أنه البيض فإنك اعتقدت الصواب

Bird Nest: Russian

Птичье гнездо

Вы когда-нибудь наблюдали, как птица вьёт гнездо? Я — да.

Сперва они находят хорошую ветвь на дереве. Она должна быть достаточно высокой, чтобы люди не смогли её достать, и достаточно крепкой, чтобы сильный ветер её не сломил.

Затем они начинают собирать палочки и кусочки ткани по всему городу. Вам, наверное, приходилось видеть летящих птиц, несущих что-то в клюве. Скорее всего, эти птицы строят гнездо.

Дальше нужно сложить палочки все вместе. Они подсовывают одну палочку сюда, другую — туда, и таким образом вскоре получается гнездо. Но это ещё не все! Дальше птицы прокладывают своё гнездо мягкими вещами, например, кусочками ткани или пуха. Некоторые птицы даже украшают свои гнёзда разными блестящими предметами.

Теперь гнездо почти готово. Осталось сделать последнее. Как по-вашему, что?

Если вы догадались, что речь идет о яйцах, то вы совершенно правы. Как только птица начинает класть яйца, значит, гнездо готово.

Bird Nest: Tagalog

Pugad ng Ibon

Nakapanood na ba kayo ng ibon na gumagawa ng pugad? Nakapanood na ako.

Una, humahanap sila ng mahusay na sanga ng punongkahoy. Ang sanga ng punongkahoy ay kailangang may sapat na taas upang hindi maabot ng manga tao at sapat ang laki upang hindi ito masira ng bagyo.

Pagkatapos ay nagtitipon sila ng manga patpat at piraso ng tela mula sa lahat ng dako ng bayan. Maaaring nakakita na kayo ng manga ibon na lumilipad na may karga sa kanilang manga tuka. Ang manga ibong ito ay malamang na gumagawa ng pugad.

Ang susunod na hakbang ay ang pagsasama-sama ng manga patpat. Itinutulak nila ang isang patpat dito at ang iba pang patpat doon at hindi magtatagal ay mayroon na silang pugad. Pero hindi pa ito tapos! Pagkatapos ay papatungan ng ibon ang pugad ng malalambot na bagay tulad ng tela o pinong balahibo. Ginagayakan pa nga ng ilang manga ibon ang kanilang pugad ng manga makikintab na bagay.

Ngayon ay halos tapos na ang pugad. Isa na lamang ang bagay na kailangan ng pugad na ito. Ano ito sa palagay ninyo?

Kung ang hula ninyo ay manga itlog, tama kayo. Kapag ang ibon ay umitlog sa pugad, ito ay tapos na.

Bird Nest: Navajo

Tsídii Bit'oh

Łahdaásh tsidii bit'oh íílééhgo yiiniłtsá? Shí éí aoo'.

Áłtsé t'iis yá'át'ééhígíí hadeentááh. T'iis deigo nineezígíí łeh diné doo deigo yííghahígíí dóó nitsaa łeh áko doo níyolgo doo k'é'éltǫǫhda.

Áadóó tsin dóó na'at'ąhí ńdayiilóóh t'áá ałtsodę́ę́'. Łahda shį́į́ tsídii yit'ahgo yiniłtsą t'áádoo le'é yótsa'go. Díí shį́į́ bit'oh íílééhgo biniinaa.

Áadóó éí tsin ahiih dayiinííł. Tsin kodę́ę́' dóó aadę́ę́' adayiiníílgo hónáásgíí at'oh yileeh. Ndi doo ałtso da. Áadóó éí tsídii t'áádoo le'é dadit'óódígíí na'at'ąhí éí doodago aghaa' ádaat'éhígíí at'oh yiih dayiiłjooł. Ła' éí tsídii t'áádoo le'é dadisxǫsígíí bit'oh yee ndeich'ąąh.

K'ad at'oh k'adę́ę́ ałtsxo'ííléé. T'áálá'ígi nááhádziih. Ha't'íísh nínízin?

Ayę́ęzhii nínízingo éí t'áá ákót'éh. Tsídii at'oh yii' ałchííhgo índa ałtsxo łeh.

The Rainy Day

It was raining and Joanne and Katy sat inside trying to come up with something to do.

"We could build a raft," suggested Joanne. It was raining so hard that building a raft almost seemed like a good idea.

"No," said Katy. "Building a raft would take too much stuff. We would need wood, nails, a hammer, and probably rope, too." Katy thought they should bake cookies.

"But we just ate lunch," said Joanne, "why don't we make paper airplanes and see whose flies the farthest?"

"That sounds like fun," said Katy, "but we can't go outside to test the airplanes and there's not enough room in here."

"Well," said Joanne, "since it's raining, why don't we put on our jackets and go splash in the puddles?"

"That's a great idea!" said Katy, and the two girls went to the closet to get their coats and boots. They buttoned their jackets, laced up their boots, and pulled down their hats around their ears.

"Are you ready?" Joanne asked.

"I sure am!" yelled Katy. She swung open the door and got ready to jump out into the rain, but when she looked up, sun was streaming through the clouds.

"I guess it's not raining any more," said Katy.

"That's right," said Joanne. "Well since it's sunny now, what do you think we should do?"

The Rainy Day: Spanish
El Día Lluvioso

Estaba lloviendo y Joanne y Katy se sentaron adentro tratando de pensar qué hacer.

"Podríamos construir una balsa", sugirió Joanne. Llovía tan fuerte que construir una balsa casi parecía una buena idea.

"No", dijo Katy. "Para construir una balsa necesitaríamos muchas cosas: madera, clavos, un martillo, y probablemente cuerda también". Katy pensó que deberían hornear galletas.

"Pero acabamos de almorzar", dijo Joanne, "¿Por qué no hacemos aviones de papel y vemos cuál vuela más lejos?"

"Buena idea", dijo Katy, "pero no podemos ir afuera para probar los aviones y aquí no hay suficiente espacio".

"Pues", dijo Joanne, "ya que está lloviendo, ¿por qué no nos ponemos la chaqueta y vamos a salpicar en los charcos?"

"¡Es una gran idea!" Dijo Kathy, y las dos niñas fueron al armario por sus abrigos y botas. Se abrocharon la chaqueta, se ataron las botas y se pusieron el sombrero tapándose las orejas.

"¿Estás lista?" preguntó Joanne..

"¡Claro que sí!", gritó Katy. Abrió la puerta y se preparó a saltar hacia la lluvia, pero cuando miró hacia arriba, el sol ya se filtraba por las nubes.

"Supongo que ya no está lloviendo", dijo Katy.

"Es cierto", dijo Joanne. "¿Bien, qué se te ocurre que hagamos ahora que hace sol?"

The Rainy Day: Vietnamese

Ngày Mưa

Trời đang mưa, Joanne và Katy ngồi trong nhà bàn tính xem nên làm gì.

"Chúng ta nên làm một cái bè đi," Joanne đề nghị. Trời mưa rất to do đó làm bè nghe có vẻ là một ý kiến hay.

"Không," Katy nói. "Làm bè sẽ cần rất nhiều thứ. Chúng ta cần gỗ, đinh, búa và có lẽ là cần dây thừng nữa." Katy nghĩ là nên cùng nhau làm bánh cookie.

"Nhưng chúng ta vừa ăn trưa mà, sao chúng ta không làm máy bay giấy và thi coi máy bay của ai bay xa nhất," Joanne nói.

"Hay quá, nhưng chúng ta không thể đi ra ngoài để thi và ở đây thì không có đủ chỗ," Katy nói.

"À, vì trời đang mưa sao chúng ta không mặc áo khoác vào và đi tóe nước trong vũng nước nhỏ?" Joanne nói.

"Thật là tuyệt vời," Katy nói. Hai cô bé đi tới tủ áo để lấy áo khoác và giày ống. Chúng gài nút áo, cột dây giày và kéo nón xuống tận vành tai.

"Bạn xong chưa?" Joanne hỏi.

"Xong rồi!" Katy la lên. Cô mở cửa ra và sẵn sàng chạy ra ngoài trời mưa, nhưng khi cô nhìn lên thì mặt trời đang chiếu qua những đám mây.

"Tôi nghĩ là trời không còn mưa nữa," Katy nói.

"Đúng rồi đó," Joanne nói. "Giờ thì trời nắng rồi, chúng ta nên làm gì hả?"

The Rainy Day: Hmong
Ib Hnub Ntuj Los Nag

Ntuj los los nag ces Joanne thiab Katy nkawd zaum hauv tsev nrhiav tswv yim saib yuav ua dab tsi.

Joanne hais tias; "Wb txua ib lub phuaj." Los nag hlob dhau ces txua ib lub phuaj xav tias yog ib lub zoo tswv yim.

Katy teb tias, "Tsi, ua phuaj yuav siv cuab yeej ntau yam heev. Wb yuav tsum muaj ntoo, ntsia thawv, rab rauj, thiab tej zaum tseem yuav tsum yuav hlua thiab." Katy xav tias tej zaum nkawd ci cookies.

"Tab sis," Joanne hais tias, "wb nyuam qhuav noj su tag ned. Tej zaum wb txiav ntawv ua nyab hoom xyuas saib leej twg lub ya mus tau deb dua?"

Katy hais tias, "Ntawd yog ib lub zoo tswv yim! Tab sis mas wb twb tawm tsis tau mus rau sab nraud kom tau sim wb cov nyab hoom thiab hauv tsev no nqaim dhau."

Joanne hais tias, "Vim ntuj los los nag ces wb kuj hnav tsho tiv nag ces wb tawm mus dhia ua si hauv cov me nyuam pas dej?"

Katy hais tias, "Ntawd yog ib lub tswv yim zoo heev li!" Ces ob tug menyuam ntxhais tau mus ntawm kem tsev muab lub tsho tiv nag thiab cov khau npuj. Nkawd khawm tsho rau, khi hlua khau npuj rau thiab rub kaum mom kom los npog nkawd cov pob ntseg.

Joanne nug tias, "Koj npaj tau lawm los?"

Katy qw hais tias, "Kuv npaj tau lawm nawj!" Nws qhib plho qhov rooj, tawm mus npaj yuav dhia mus tiv nag, tab sis nws tig ntsia saum ntuj nav has hnub twb ci tshab cov huab tuaj.

Katy hais tias, "Kuv xav tias ntuj tsis los nag lawm."

"Yog kawg," Joanne hais tias. "Tam sis no ntuj tsis los nag lawm, koj xav tias wb yuav ua dab tsi?"

The Rainy Day: Traditional Chinese Script

下雨天

　　天正在下雨，瓊安和凱蒂坐在屋內，並絞盡腦汁想要做些什麼。

　　「我們可以蓋一個竹筏。」瓊安建議說。雨下得那麼大，蓋一個竹筏聽起來像是一個好主意。

　　「不，蓋竹筏需要太多東西。我們需要木頭、釘子、榔頭，還可能需要 繩子。」凱蒂說。凱蒂認爲她們應該烘烤餅乾。

　　「可是我們剛剛吃了午飯。我們何不做一些紙飛機，然後看誰的飛機飛得 最遠？」瓊安說。

　　「這真是個好主意。可是我們不能到外頭試飛機，而且這裡地方又不大。」凱蒂說。

　　「那麼，既然在下雨，我們何不穿上外套，到水坑跳著玩呢？」瓊安說。

　　「那實在是一個好主意。」凱蒂說。於是兩個女孩到衣櫃拿她們的大衣和 長筒靴。她們扣好扣子，繫上靴帶，把帽子拉下蓋住耳朵。

　　「你準備好了嗎？」瓊安問。

　　「我當然準備好了！」凱蒂叫喊著。她敞開大門，準備跳進雨中。可是當她擡頭看時，陽光正從朵朵雲彩照射下來。

　　「我想現在已經不再下雨了。」凱蒂說。

　　「是的。既然現在太陽出來了，那你想我們該做什麼呢？」瓊安問道。

The Rainy Day: Korean

비오는 날

비가 오고 있었습니다. 조앤과 케이티는 집 안에 앉아서, 무엇을 할까 곰곰히 생각하고 있었습니다.

"우리는 뗏목을 만들 수 있어." 조앤이 제의했습니다. 비가 많이 오고 있어서 뗏목을 만드는 것은 좋은 생각 같았습니다.

"아니야, 뗏목을 만들려면 필요한 물건이 너무 많아. 나무, 못, 망치가 필요하고, 어쩌면 밧줄도 필요할 수 있어"라고 케이티가 말했습니다. 케이티는 쿠키를 굽는 것이 좋겠다고 생각했습니다.

"하지만 우린 방금 점심을 먹었잖아. 종이 비행기를 접어서 누구 것이 더 멀리 나는지 던져보는 것이 어때?"라고 조앤이 말했습니다.

"그것 참 좋은 생각이야. 하지만 밖에 나가서 비행기를 날릴 수도 없고 집안은 공간이 부족해"라고 케이티가 말했습니다.

"그렇다면 이왕에 비가 내리고 있으니까, 외투를 입고 웅덩이에 가서 뛰면서 물장난을 하는 것이 어때?"라고 조앤이 말했습니다.

"그것 참 기발한 생각이야"이라고 케이티가 말했습니다. 두 소녀는 외투와 장화를 가지러 옷장에 갔습니다. 둘은 외투의 단추를 잠그고 장화의 끈을 매고 모자를 내려 귀까지 덮었습니다.

"준비 다 됐니?"라고 조앤이 물었습니다.

The Rainy Day: Haitian Creole
Jou lapli a

Li t ap fè lapli epi Joanne ak Katy te chita andedan an pandan yo t ap eseye deside ki sa pou yo fè.

"Nou te ka bati yon rado," Joanne te sijere. Lapli a t ap tonbe sitèlman fò li te sanble se te yon bon lide pou bati yon rado.

"Non," Katy di. "Sa pral mande twòp bagay pou bati yon rado. Nou ta va bezwen bwa, klou, yon mato, epi petèt yon kòd tou." Katy te panse yo ta dwe kwit bonbon depreferans.

"Men nou fèk manje lench," Joanne di, "poukisa nou pa fè kèk avyon an papye epi wè kiyès ladan yo ki ka vole pi lwen ?"

"Se yon ide mayifik," Katy di, "men nou paka ale deyò a pou teste avyon yo epi pa gen ase plas andedan an."

"Ebyen," Joanne di, "piske l ap fè lapli, poukisa nou pa mete manto nou sou nou epi ale jwe nan ma dlo yo ?"

"Se yon bon ide !" Katy di, epi de tifi yo te ale nan amwa yo pou yo pran manto yo ak bòt yo. Yo te boutonnen manto yo, lase bòt yo epi rale chapo yo desann bò zòrèy yo.

"Èske w prè ?" Joanne mande.

"Byensi mwen prè !" Katy reponn byen fò. Li ouvè pòt la epi li prepare l pou l soti nan lapli a, men lè li voye je l gade anlè, solèy la t ap reyone nan nyaj yo.

"Mwen sipoze li pap fè lapli ankò," Katy di.

"Se vre," Joanne di. "Ebyen piske solèy la deyò kounye a, ki sa w panse nou dwe fè ?"

The Rainy Day: Arabic

لايوم الممطر

و كان يوماً ممطراً و جوان" و"كيتي" يجلسون بداخل المنزل
نستطيع أن نبني طوف". اقترحت. إ.عملهم يميف اميف يتشاورون نحن, "جوان",
كانت فكرة جيدة.
كانت تمطر بشدة وبناء الطوف . "فوط نبني نأ عيطتسن

سوف نحتاج خشب، ومسامير، ومطرأضيا، وحبل، وقة." فكرت بانءاعطوف ال بانطلب أشياء كثيرة.
كاتي" بان تخبز البسكويت.

قالت "جوان", "ولكننا نهتنا من اكل الغداء" لماذا ال نعمل
طائرات ورقية ولرنى أي طائرة ستطير لمسافة أبعد؟"

ولكن ليس باستطاعتنا الخروج لإختبار " ، "كاتي فكرت فكرة رائعة" ، "كاتي
المكان هنا ليس متسعاً بما فيه الطائرات والمكان هنا ليس متسعاً بما فيه الكافية".

قالت "جوان", "حسناً" ، " مب امن إنا لمطر ال نلبس معاطفنا
ونخرج نلعب ب في امكان الميه المتجمعة؟".

قالت "كاتي", "هذه فكرة عظيمة" ، وذهبت البنتين إلى إ
الولد بالحضار المعاطف فـ والاحذية. لبست البنات معاطفهم
، وربطوا احذيتهم وشدوا قباعتهم إلى السفل فوق قوذانهم.

"سألت جوان "هل انت جاهزة؟",
"قالت "كاتي", "نعم بالتأكيد". وفتحت الباب على
مصراعيه واستعدت للقفز إلى الخارج في المطر، ولكن
عندما نظرت إلى أعلى، كانت اشعة الشمس تتسلل من بين
السحاب.

"كاتي" قالت أعتقد ان المطر قد توقفت.
قالت "جوان" اذه صحيح". و ماذا تعتقدين أن نفعل؟ ساطعة الآن
"حسناً، بما أن الشمس

The Rainy Day: Russian

Дождливый день

Лил дождь, и Джоанна с Кэти сидели дома и думали, чем бы заняться.

«Может, построить плот?» — предложила Джоанна. Дождь был такой сильный, что постройка плота показалась не такой уж плохой идеей.

«Нет, — ответила Кэти. — Для этого нам слишком много надо: доски, гвозди, молоток и ещё, наверное, верёвки». Кэти считала, что лучше им испечь печенье.

«Но ведь мы только что пообедали, — возразила Джоанна. — Давай лучше сделаем бумажные самолётики и посмотрим, чей дальше полетит?»

«Это, конечно, замечательно, но мы не сможем выйти на улицу, чтобы их запустить, а тут места совсем мало».

«Ну, если уж идет дождь, давай просто наденем куртки и пойдём погуляем, пошлёпаем по лужам», — предложила Джоанна.

«Хорошая мысль!» — сказала Кэти, и обе девочки пошли надевать куртки и ботинки. Они застегнули куртки, зашнуровали ботинки и натянули шапки на самые уши.

«Готова?» — спросила Джоанна.

«Конечно!» — крикнула Кэти. Как только она распахнула дверь и приготовилась выпрыгнуть наружу, она обнаружила, что солнце пробивается сквозь тучи.

«По-моему, дождь кончился», — сказала Кэти.

«Точно, — ответила Джоанна. — Светит солнце. Как ты думаешь, чем бы нам теперь заняться?»

The Rainy Day: Tagalog
Araw na Maulan

Umuulan at sina Joanne at Katy ay nakaupo sa loob at nag-iisip ng magagawa.

"Maaari tayong gumawa ng balsa," mungkahi ni Joanne. Napakalakas ng ulan kaya ang paggawa ng balsa ay anyong magandang ideya.

"Hindi," sabi ni Katy. "Ang paggawa ng balsa ay mgangailangan ng napakaraming bagay. Kakailanganin natin ng kahoy, manga pako, isang martilyo, at malamang ay lubid din." Naisip ni Katy na gumawa sila ng cookies.

"Pero katatapos pa lamang nating kumain ng tanghalian," sabi ni Joanne, "bakit hindi tayo gumawa ng manga papel na eruplano at tingnan kung kanino ang makakalipad nang pinakamalayo?"

"Iyan ay magandang ideya," sabi ni Katy, "pero hindi tayo makakalabas upang subukan ang manga eruplano at walang sapat na lugar rito."

"Buweno," sabi ni Joanne, "dahil umuulan, bakit hindi natin isuot ang ating manga dyaket at tumalun-talon sa manga sanaw?"

"Magandang ideya 'yan!" sabi ni Katy, at ang dalawang babae ay nagpunta sa aparador upang kunin ang kanilang manga dyaket at bota. Ibinutones nila ang kanilang manga dyaket, tinalian ang kanilang manga bota at ibinaba ang kanilang manga sumbrero sa kanilang manga tainga.

"Handa ka na ba?" itinanong ni Joanne.

"Handang-handa na!" sigaw ni Katy. Binuksan niya ang pinto at naghandang lumundag sa ulan, pero nang tumingala siya, ang araw ay sumisinag sa manga ulap.

"Hindi na pala umuulan," sabi ni Katy.

"Oo nga," sabi ni Joanne. "Dahil hindi na umuulan, ano sa palagay mo ang dapat nating gawin?"

The Rainy Day: Navajo

Nahałtin

Nahałtingo Joanne dóó Katy kóne' siké ha'át'íí lá baa ndiit'ash nízingo.

Tsin naa'eełí daats'í la' ádiilnííł ní Joanne. Ayóó nahałtingo biniinaa tsin naa'eeł álnééhgo beelt'é nízin.

Dooda ní Katy. Tsin naa'eeł íílnééhgo t'áádoo le'é t'óó ahayóígo choo'į̃. Tsineeshjį̃į̃' dóó bił adaalkaałí dóó bee adaalkaałí dóó tl'óół shį̃į̃. Katy éí t'óó bááh dá'áka'í ádiilnííł nízin.

Índa yee' iidą́ą́' ní Joanne. Naaltsoos naat'a'ígo shą́' ádiilnííł dóó háí bíhígíí alááhdi naat'a' doo ní.

Jó éí nizhóní ní Katy. Ndi tł'óó'góó doo bii ghah da dóó kóne' doo haz'ą́ą da.

Iishją́ą́ shį̃į̃ ní Joanne. Nahałtin dą́ą́' nihi'éétsoh biih diit'ash dóó tó bii' nei'née doo.

Jó éí nizhóní, ní Katy áádóó at'ééké bi'éétsoh dóó bikee nineezígíí néídiinil. Bi'éétsoh yił dah aznil dóó bikee' ye'eztł'ǫ́ dóó bich'ah áyiilaa bijaa' bik'ésti'go.

K'adísh ní Joanne.

Aoo' ní Katy. Dáádílkał ą̨ą'áyiilaa dóó ch'íhi'neelchééh n̨t'éé' ch'í'ní'ą̨ą lá k'os bitahdę́ę́.

Doo nahałtin da lá k'ad ní Katy.

Ei lą́ą ní Joanne. Jó k'ad ch'í'ní'ą̨adą́ą́' ha'ąt'íísh baa ndiit'ash nínízin?

References

Flannery, M. E. (2006). Language can't be a barrier. *NEA Today*, 24(4), 24–30.

Greenberg, E., Reynaldo, F. M., Rhodes, D., & Chan, T. (2001). English literacy and language minorities in the United States. *Education Statistics Quarterly, 3*(4), 73–75.

Grimmett, B. F. (2003). *Being Hmong in America: Hmong American organizations and the reclaiming of a lost culture.* Boston: Harvard Divinity School; The Pluralism Project.

Meyer, D., Madden, D., & McGrath, D. (2004). English language learner students in U.S. public schools: 1994 and 2000. *Education Statistics Quarterly, 6*(3). Retrieved September 30, 2007, from http://nces.ed.gov/programs/quarterly/vol_6/6_3/3_4.asp

Mote, S. M. (2004). *Hmong and American: Stories of transition to a strange land.* Jefferson, NC: McFarland & Company, Inc.

Northwest Regional Educational Laboratory. (2003). *General principles for teaching ELL students.* Retrieved January 3, 2006, from http://www.nwrel.org/request/2003may/general.html

Ortiz, F. I. (1995). Mexican American women: Schooling, work, and family. *ERIC Digest.* (ERIC Document Reproduction Services No. ED388490) http://www.eric.ed.gov/ERICWebPortal/Home.portal

Padolsky, D. (2005). *How has the English language learner population changed in recent years?* OELA's National Clearinghouse for English Language Acquisition and Language Instruction Educational Programs. Retrieved December 11, 2005, from http://www.ncela.gwu.edu/new/whatsnewold.html

Tso, Betty. (n.d.) Land is holy. In *Navajo religion: A sacred way of life.* Retrieved September 25, 2007, from http://www.xpressweb.com/zionpark/index3.html

U.S. Census Bureau. (2007) *American Community Survey Data Profile Highlights.* Retrieved September 30, 2007, from http://factfinder.census.gov/home/saff/main.html?_lang=en

Weaver, A. (2005, October 23). Bee Xiong's first day of school challenging. Manitowoc, *Wisconsin Herald Times*, p. C4.

Additional Resources

American Religion Data Archive. (2002). *Religious affiliations, 2000: Navajo County, Arizona.* Retrieved December 15, 2005, from http://www.thearda.com/index.asp

Baker, H., & Ho, P. K. (2003) *Teach yourself Cantonese.* New York: McGraw Hill, 2003.

Bernstein, R., & Bergman. M. (2003). *Annual demographic supplement to the March 2002 Current Population Survey.* Washington, DC: U. S. Census Bureau.

Brittingham, A., & de la Cruz, P. G. (2005). *We the people of Arab ancestry in the United States* (CENSR-21). Washington, DC: U.S. Census Bureau.

Chen, J., & Simms, E. (2005) *A practical Chinese-English pronouncing dictionary.* North Clarendon, VT: Charles E. Tuttle Co.

Claudio-Perez, M. (1998). *Filipino Americans.* California State Library. Retrieved December 10, 2005, from http://www.library.ca.gov/index.html

Echevarria, J., Vogt, M., & Short, D. (2003). *Making content comprehensible for English language learners: The SIOP model.* Boston: Allyn & Bacon.

Enriquez, L., & Pajewski, A. (1996). Teaching from a Hispanic perspective: A handbook for non-Hispanic adult educators. *LiteracyNet.* Retrieved December 19, 2005, from http://www.literacynet.org/lp/hperspectives

Factbook. (2005). *Philippines.* Retrieved December 10, 2005, from https://www.cia.gov/library/publications/the-world-factbook/index.html

Fay, K. (2006). Tips for teaching. *NEA Today, 24*(4), 28.

Goosen, I. (1995). *Diné bizaad: Speak, read, write Navajo.* Flagstaff, AZ: Salina Bookshelf.

Harrell, A., & Jordan, M. (2003) *Fifty strategies for teaching English language learners.* Englewood Cliffs, NJ: Prentice Hall.

Immigration: Polish/Russian. The American Memory Project: Library of Congress. (2004). Retrieved December 6, 2005, from http://www.memory.loc.gov/learn/features/immig/polish.html

Kibria, N. (2002). *Becoming Asian American.* Baltimore: The Johns Hopkins University Press.

Kottler, E., & Kottler, J. (2001). *Children with limited English: Teaching strategies for the regular classroom.* Thousand Oaks, CA: Corwin Press.

Louie, A. (2004). *Chineseness across borders.* Durham, NC: Duke University Press.

Minato, R. (2005). *Filipino Americans.* The Washington State Commission on Asian Pacific American Affairs. Retrieved December 9, 2005, from http://www.capaa.wa.gov

National Clearinghouse for English Language Acquisition and Language Instruction Educational Programs (NCELA). (2006, November). How has the English language learner population changed in recent years? (NCELA FAQs). Retrieved October 1, 2007, from http://www.ncela.gwu.edu/expert/faq/08leps.html

Newland, K., & Grieco, E. (2004). Spotlight on Haitians in the United States. *US in Focus.* Retrieved December, 5, 2005, from http://www.migrationinformation.org/index.cfm?

Northern Illinois University and the Center for Southeast Asian Studies. (2005). *Tagalog: Interactive language and Filipino culture resources*. Retrieved December 10, 2005, from http://www.seasite.niu.edu/Tagalog/Tagalog_mainpage.htm

Pimsleur Language Programs. *Chinese (Cantonese)*.(1999). Philadelphia: Author.

Pitton, D., Warring, D., Frank, K., & Hunter, S. (1993). Multicultural Messages: Nonverbal Communication in the Classroom. *Resources in Education*. (ERIC Document Reproduction Service No. ED 362519)

Topics Entertainment. (2004). *Talk now! Learn Navajo* [CD-ROM]. Renton, WA: Author.

U.S. Census Bureau. (2005). *State and County QuickFacts: Navajo County Arizona*. Retrieved December 13, 2005, from quickfacts.census.gov/qfd/states/04/04017.html

U.S. Library of Congress. (1998). *Country studies: Haiti*. Retrieved December 5, 2005, from http://www.countrystudies.us/

Villereal, G., & Cavazos, A. (2005). Shifting identity: Process and change in identity of aging Mexican-American males. *Journal of Sociology and Social Welfare*, *32*(1), 33-41.

Wilson, A. (1992). *Breakthrough Navajo: An introductory course*. Madison, CT: Audio Forum.

Zhou, M. & Bankston, C.L. (1998). *Growing Up American*. New York: Russell Sage Foundation.

CORWIN PRESS

The Corwin Press logo—a raven striding across an open book—represents the union of courage and learning. Corwin Press is committed to improving education for all learners by publishing books and other professional development resources for those serving the field of PreK–12 education. By providing practical, hands-on materials, Corwin Press continues to carry out the promise of its motto: **"Helping Educators Do Their Work Better."**